The Iditarod
Women on the Trail

By Nicki J. Nielsen

Wolfdog Publications
Anchorage, Alaska

Copyright © 1986
Nicki J. Nielsen

Wolfdog Publications
P.O. Box 142506
Anchorage, Alaska 99514-2506

Library of Congress Catalog Number: 85-52335
International Standard Book Number: 0-9616191-0-4

First Edition, February 1986

Cover artist: Rose Albert

Typesetting by Visible Ink, Inc.
Anchorage, AK

Cover printed by L & B Color Printing
Wasilla, AK

Printing by Thompson Printing Service.
Anchorage, AK

Printed in the United States of America

All rights reserved. No part of this publication may be reproduced or transmitted in any form or by any means, electronic or mechanical, including photocopy, recording, or any other information retrieval system without permission in writing of the author, except for short excerpts in reviews or scholarly works.

Dedication

This book is dedicated to all the dog mushers who take to the trails to enjoy the peace and beauty of Alaska's countryside. It is especially dedicated to those women who have run the Iditarod race and who plan to run it.

Acknowledgements

A special thanks is owed to the women who have run in the Iditarod race to Nome for their willingness to share their experiences with me. Contact was made with each one of them. I appreciate very much their willingness to review the material included here, which has been invaluable in helping insure accuracy of the facts as they have related them.

Many friends have encouraged me to undertake this project and have given me invaluable help. Gene Gilman, Iditarod volunteer extraordinary, was instrumental in urging me to do this project. Vi Redington, wife of Joe Redington Sr., "Father of the Iditarod," provided helpful background information about the events leading up to the early Iditarod Trail races. Robert L. Spude generously allowed me to summarize material from his excellent historical overview of the Iditarod Trail and its relationship within Alaska's history. I am grateful to the following individuals who have read and commented on parts of the text: Thelma Langdon, Donald Sparrow, Norma Hoyt, and Joan Johnson. Various staff members of the Iditarod Trail Committee have helped me by providing information which enabled me to locate some of the earlier mushers, as have other individuals too numerous to thank individually.

I am especially grateful to my husband, Bob, for his patience and help in many areas. He helped take photographs, proof read text, and gave valuable editorial input.

I am grateful to all the mushers who provided photographs for this book. Thanks is owed to Verda Carey of the Alaska Historical Library for her help in locating a number of early photographs; to Mary Fechner of the Anchorage Museum; and to Jim Brown, an official photographer for the Iditarod Trail Committee. Most photographs are noted as to source. Those not specifically noted were taken by the author or her husband.

A note on the organization of this book is in order. Each musher's sketch or profile is arranged in order of the first year she raced and her final position in that race. All quotations, unless specifically footnoted, come from interviews, conversations, and correspondence with the mushers.

Foreword

Nicki Nielsen has undertaken and completed a project long overdue. She has interviewed and written about each woman who has entered the Iditarod Trail race since the first race to Nome in 1973. She included not only those who completed the race, but all those who entered or started.

The book is a tribute to the courage and dedication of the women who have challenged the Iditarod, "The Last Great Race," — and won or lost that challenge. It is also a tribute to Libby Riddles, of Teller, Alaska, who was the first woman to win the Iditarod race. The 1985 champion has been an inspiration to women all over the world.

Vi Redington & Dorothy Page

The Iditarod Trail Sled Dog Race

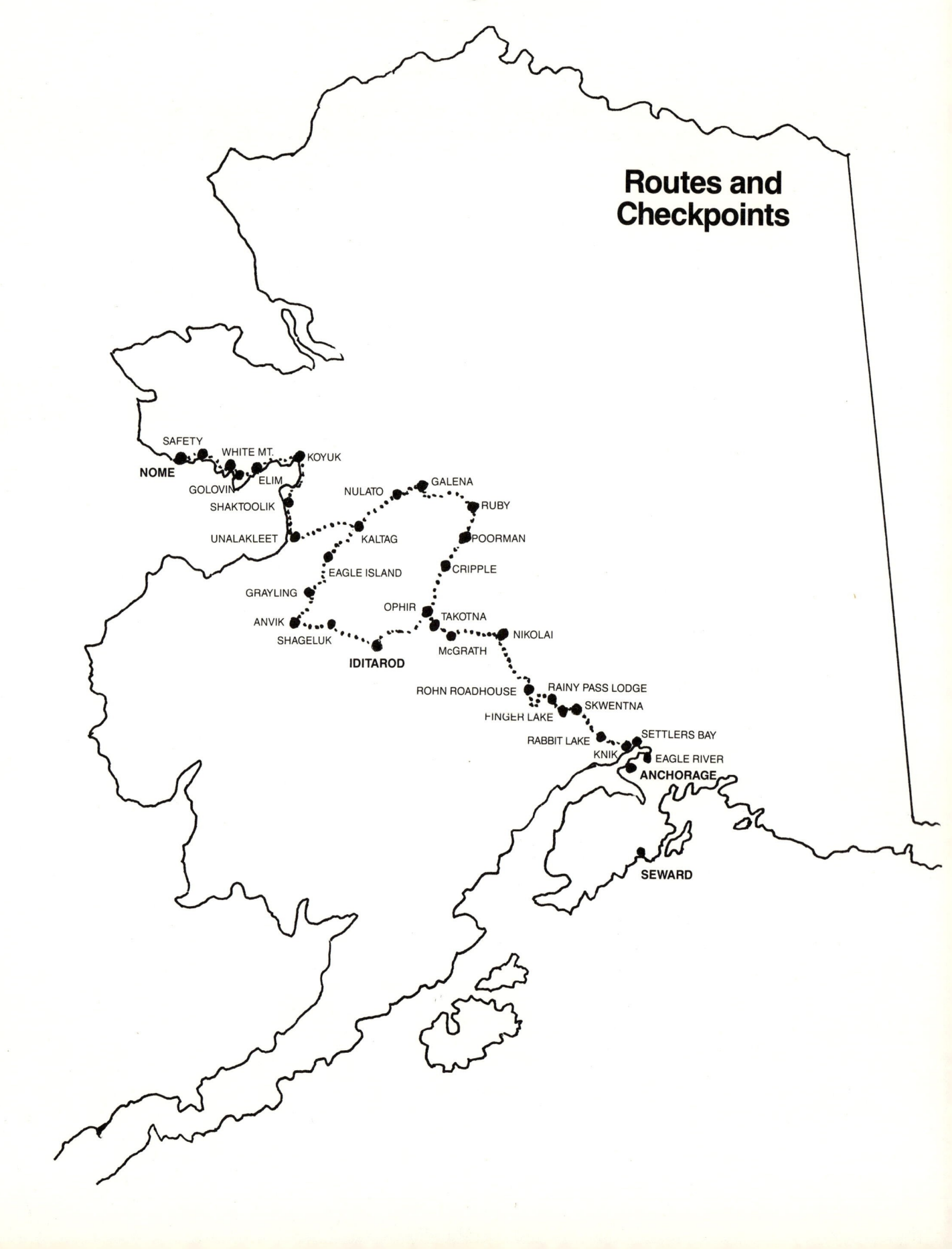

Routes and Checkpoints

Table of Contents

Chapter 1: The Historical Setting 3
Background
Reminiscences of Travelers along the Iditarod Trail

Chapter 2: Sled Dog Races Along the Iditarod Trail 9
Early Races
The Iditarod Race

Chapter 3: Women in the Iditarod Race: The Pioneers 1974-1977 15
Mary Shields, Lolly Medley, Ginger Burcham,
Varona Thompson, Dinah Knight

Chapter 4: New Women Entrants: 1978-1980. 23
Susan Butcher, Shelley Gill Vandiver, Patty Friend,
Donna Gentry, Libby Riddles, Dee Dee Jonrowe,
Marjorie Moore, Barbara Moore

Chapter 5: New Women Entrants: 1981-1983 41
Sue Firmin, Rose Albert, Roxy Wright, Shannon Poole,
Christine O'Gar, Connie Frerichs, Fritz Kirsch, Pam Flowers,
Beverly Jerue Masek

Chapter 6: New Women Entrants: 1984-1985 55
Diana Dronenburg, Kari Skogen, Francine Bennis, Miki Collins,
Betsy McGuire, Claire Philip, Monique Bene

Chapter 7: 1986 Entrants 65

Women's Race Statistics 67

Footnotes 68

Bibliography 69

Glossary 70

Index 71

Above, man with dog team, freighting supplies. Author's collection.

Left, traveling along the Iditarod Trail route on rail trestle north of Seward. Postcard, author's collection.

Mining in the Iditarod district. Lomen Bros. photo postcard, author's collection.

CHAPTER 1

The Historical Setting

The Iditarod, Alaska's last major gold rush, covered a large area. Prospectors arrived in the late 1880s, and minor stampedes occurred up to 1907 with strikes on Ganes Creek and near Ophir. Between 1910 and 1912 the rush to Iditarod and Ruby brought over 10,000 stampeders. Over $30 million in gold was taken out within two decades.[1]

Its location in Interior Alaska isolated the Iditarod District except for summer access by meandering river routes between May and October. Between January and April 1908 W.L. Goodwin completed a winter reconnaissance from Seward to Nome for the Alaska Road Commission, blazing a winter trail.[2] This trail, which he surveyed and blazed again from Nome to Seward in 1910-1911,[3] became known as the Iditarod Trail. It became the main winter access route to the Iditarod District. Many people either walked it or mushed it with dog teams. Since the late 1920s, due to the use of the airplane, it has been used mainly for local travel.

In 1973 an Iditarod Trail Sled Dog Race was held from Anchorage to Nome, a distance of over 1,000 miles. This race, held annually, now alternates years between a northern and southern trail route. Billed as a 1,049 mile race, the 1,049 stands for the distance of over 1,000 miles and the 49 represents the 49th state.

This book focuses on the women who have run in the Iditarod race. A profile of each female musher is included. The individual women are placed in chapters based on which year they first ran the race. Their placement within that year they first ran is done in numerical order of their finishing position. All quotations not footnoted come from interviews, conversations, or correspondence with the mushers themselves.

Much of the information in the background section which follows, unless otherwise footnoted, is summarized from Robert L. Spude, Historic Overview, in *The Iditarod National Historic Trail*, published in 1981 by the Bureau of Land Management.

BACKGROUND

The Iditarod National Historic Trail holds a unique place in Alaskan and American history. A product of the Alaskan Gold Rush Era, this winter trail connected mining camps, trading posts and Native villages in Alaska's Interior. It incorporated the Native Indian and Eskimo trails. These early Alaskan Natives had used dogsleds and snowshoes to travel during the long winters when rivers and streams were frozen.

Our stereotyped image of the parka-clad musher traveling behind a sled driven by a string of dogs reflects a blend of Native and Russian influence. The natives built sleds to carry possessions from camp to camp or camp to village. The owner ran in front of the sled guiding his dog team along the unimproved trail. As early as the 1840s Lt. Zagoskin, a Russian, wrote about his countrymen introducing harnessing dogs in pairs or single file in front of a sled. The Russians also introduced the use of the best trained dog or "leader" (lead dog) who recognized voice commands for direction, and who kept the other dogs in line. Later in the Russian era, first guide poles and later handlebars were attached to the rear of the sled to direct, push, and balance the weight.

The Russians also developed parts of what later became the Iditarod Trail as routes for supplying fur trading posts. Trading expeditions went across the Kaltag Portage to Nulato on the Yukon River, along a section on which the Iditarod Trail was later built.

Alaska's Gold Rush came much later than the frontier mining eras of other western states. As those frontiers closed people wandered further north to prospect, to trap, and to trade. Many of these individuals moved up the Pacific Coast with the series of strikes. In the 1880s some crossed to the Yukon River while others continued along the coast. The different conditions of geography and northern climate gave way to new adaptations. Dogs and sleds replaced the burro, and sourdough replaced johnny cakes.

The Cook Inlet country was the first mining area to develop along the future route of the Iditarod Trail. Numerous bays and streams resulted from where the glacial Chugach and Kenai ranges cut along the Inlet's shores. Rich pockets of gold were deposited in some of these streams. Although the Russians and early traders had found traces of gold, no major finds were made until 1891.

In 1891 Al King, a veteran prospector from the interior, located gold on Resurrection Creek which flowed into Turnagain Arm. Working with a gold pan and rocker, he kept his find secret. 1895-1896 was boom time for the newly established Turnagain Mining District. Rich finds on the tributaries of Six Mile, Resurrection, and Glacier Creeks brought 3,000 people to the area. During the 1890s roughly blazed trails connected Sunrise, Hope, and scattered trading posts at Resurrection Bay, Knik Arm, and the Susitna River.

The miners followed the seasons. After freeze up in the fall they hooked up their dogs and pulled their sleds loaded with a year or two of supplies up the rivers to promising locations. They spent winters thawing ground and digging gravel. At breakup in the spring the plentiful supply of water was used to sluice the pay dirt in search of gold. At the end of the summer they built rafts and poling boats and floated downstream to towns or trading posts.

The 1896 Canadian Klondike Gold Rush provided the greatest impetus to gold mining in Alaska of any event to date. The 1897-1898 stampede brought an estimated 50,000 hopeful persons North. Many never reached the Klondike. Some settled in Cook Inlet. Others went to areas along the American side of the Yukon River or elsewhere in Alaska's Interior.

In 1898 gold was discovered on the shores of the Bering Sea at Anvil Creek. The town of Nome, Alaska sprang up overnight. By the summer of 1900 upwards of 30,000 people arrived to dig the sands of Nome's beaches. From October to June the Bering Sea was frozen, as were the great inland waterways of the Yukon River and other rivers and streams. Those who missed the last steamers out of Alaska in October were isolated for the winter. A telegraph system was constructed across Alaska from Valdez to Nome. Trails were cleared to bring in supplies and the mail. All winter mail to and from Nome in 1904-1905 went via Valdez and Fairbanks.

From 1898 to 1908 several routes connected ice free ports with Nome. The first went from Skagway, Alaska to Dawson, Yukon Territory, and along the Yukon River to the Bering Sea coast and on to Nome. Since it crossed through Canada on its 2,000 plus mile journey, it was unsatisfactory to those wishing an all American route. A Valdez to Eagle Trail and thence west down the Yukon River proved uneconomical. After the Fairbanks, Alaska, Gold Rush in 1903 the Valdez route via Fairbanks and the Yukon River became feasible.

It was believed that a Cook Inlet route to Nome would be the shortest route. Construction of a railroad north from Seward started in 1904. (It later became part of the present Alaska Railroad.) In 1907, due to the development of the town of Seward on Resurrection Bay and recent gold discoveries in the Innoko District, the Army's Alaska Road Commission, under Major Wilds P. Richardson, ordered Walter Goodwin and a crew of three to blaze a route from Seward through Cook Inlet country to Nome.

Number 5, Anvil Creek, one of the richest placer claims in Nome. Author's collection.

Goodwin's blazed and cleared winter trail to Nome, later called the Iditarod Trail, became the main winter trail to the Iditarod District. A loop trail followed the creeks to the town of Iditarod, and then north to later rejoin the main trail. A trail went to Ruby on the Yukon River. At Ruby one could go east to Fairbanks or west to Nome. Most travelers along the Iditarod Trail did not go the entire route to Nome. Instead, they traveled from Seward to the various mining districts, or used segments of the trail while traveling between mining camps and trade centers.

Many people *walked* the trail. The heroes of the trail, however, were the dogsled team and driver. Roadhouses lined the trail and its branches. They were located at intervals of about twenty miles, approximately a one day journey. Accommodations varied. Many had dog barns and horse stables. Some were very inferior in service and accommodations. Others were clean, comfortable, and very hospitable. All roadhouses were required to keep lists of travelers in order to facilitate finding the last known location of lost individuals. Territorial funds were set aside for staking trails and building shelter cabins to save the lives of travelers stranded by blizzards.

World War I brought the days of isolation closer to their end. Young miners and workers enlisted in the service and left the Territory. Most never returned. The 1920s changed life in the remote areas of Alaska greatly. In February 1924 the first mail was officially carried by airplane from Fairbanks to McGrath in Alaska's Interior. By the late 1920s the airplane replaced the dog team in most of Interior Alaska.

The use of the Iditarod Trail and dog teams faded into history. Before this occurred, the single most publicized dog sled delivery took place. The year was 1925. Nome was threatened by a diphtheria epidemic. Serum supplies were low. A wire was sent requesting serum be rushed to Nome. Due to the extremely cold weather conditions and the lack of winter airplane experience, it was decided to send the serum by dog team. Packaged to prevent it from freezing, the serum was placed on the Alaska Railroad at Anchorage for the trip to Nenana. Along the frozen winter trails a team of relay drivers was gathered to mush the serum by dog team from Nenana to Nome as quickly as possible. Twenty mushers carried the serum 674 miles to Nome in 127½ hours.[4] The threatened epidemic was averted.

The lead dog on the last leg of the trip, Balto, was immortalized by having a statue cast of him which stands today in New York City's Central Park.[5]

Leonhard Seppala, Charles Evans, Edgar Nollner, Bill McCarty and Edgar Kallands were among those hardy mushers. The starting number one position in the Iditarod Trail Sled Dog Race was reserved for one of these mushers from its start in 1967 as a shorter Alaska Purchase Centennial Race through the 1973 to 1984 races.

Above, Canton's Pioneer Roadhouse, Knik, Alaska. The Anchorage Museum of History and Art.

Below, travelers along the trail near Knik. Note "Cottonwood Road House" sign. The Anchorage Museum of History and Art.

Clough's Roadhouse on the Iditarod Trail near McGrath. Postcard, author's collection.

REMINISCENCES OF TRAVELERS ALONG THE IDITAROD TRAIL

The original trail began in Seward and followed the tracks of the old Alaska Central Railway (later the Alaska Railroad) to the end of the tracks (mile 54 at the time of Goodwin's 1908 survey). It then went via Turnagain Arm, Glacier Creek, Crow Pass, Eagle River, across country to Old Knik (now Eklutna), and across Knik Arm to New Knik. It continued across country to Susitna Station, up the Susitna three miles, up the Yentna, Skwentna and Happy Rivers, Pass Creek to Rainy Pass, down the Dalzell, Rohn and Kuskokwim Rivers to near the Tonzona. It then went to the mouth of the Takotna at McGrath, up the Takotna and across country to the Takotna Slough, over rolling hills to Ganes Creek, down Ganes Creek and across country to Ophir Creek (the Innoko District) to Dishakaket, across country to Kaiyuk [sic] Slough to the Yukon, then up the Yukon to Kaltag, and then by the overland mail trail via Unalakleet to Nome.[6]

Charles Lee Cadwallader, in his monograph, *Reminiscences of the Iditarod Trail*,[7] describes his experiences going in and out over the Iditarod Trail in 1917 and 1919. He *walked* much of the trail. Some quotes are presented to give a feeling for travel on the trail from Knik to Iditarod.

April 2, 1917: Left Knik "at 4:00 P.M. started for the Little Susitna Roadhouse, 14 miles away . . . . We arrived at . . . 9:00 P.M."

April 3: "Left the Little Susitna Roadhouse 9:00 A.M. . . . . The trail was good and the sun was out . . . . Arrived Susitna Roadhouse 1:00 P.M., 14 miles."

April 5: "Left Lakeview 7:00 A.M., 18 miles . . . began to feel the soreness in all my leg muscles . . . . Arrived 1:30 P.M. at Skwentna Crossing Roadhouse." (Cadwallader is *walking* the trail!)

April 6: "Left Skwentna Crossing Roadhouse 6:15 A.M., 21 miles. Arrived Mountain Climbers Roadhouse 1:00 P.M. . . . . The snow was nine feet deep."

April 7: "Left Mountain Climbers' Roadhouse 5:30 A.M., arrived at Happy River Roadhouse 11:00 A.M., 22 miles . . . at the foot of the steep climb going over the Alaska Range."

April 8: "Left Happy River Roadhouse 5:45 A.M., arrived Rainy Pass Roadhouse 1:25 P.M., 30 miles. The climb was pretty steep all the way to the timber line . . . we crossed a couple of small lakes and they were not frozen over . . . . It was here that a musher had disappeared from his associates a year previous while coming out over the trail."

April 9: "Left Rainy Pass Roadhouse 5:00 A.M., arrived Rhone River Roadhouse 11:30 A.M., 28 miles . . . all of us felt like making the next Roadhouse, French Joe's. Left . . . 3:10 P.M., arrived at Pioneer Roadhouse at 9:30 P.M., 16 miles. This is a 44 mile mush — was accomplished with less fatigue than the second day out when we only made 14 miles."

April 10: "Left French Joe's Pioneer Roadhouse at 9:00 A.M., arrived Peluk Roadhouse 3:15 P.M., 20 miles . . . over rolling country in the Valley of the Kuskokwim River."

April 11: "Left Peluk Roadhouse 5:30 A.M., arrived Salmon River Roadhouse 11:30 A.M., 20 miles. "The Turk" sure put out hotcakes that were hard to improve on, and he had a lot of fun doing and talking about it."

April 12: "Left the Salmon River Roadhouse 5:30 A.M., arrived at Big River Roadhouse 1:30 P.M., 28 miles. At this point the soreness has all gone from my legs and hips."

April 13: "Left Big River Roadhouse 5:30 A.M., arrived McGrath Roadhouse 9:00 A.M., 10 miles. Left McGrath Roadhouse 9:30 A.M. . . . . Arrived at Takotna Roadhouse 2:20 P.M., 19 miles."

April 14: "Left Takotna Roadhouse 6:20 A.M., arrived Ophir Roadhouse 1:20 P.M. Ophir had quite a bit of activity for this time of year. There was a crew of men taking out a winter's dump on Ophir Creek . . . ."

April 15: "Left Ophir Roadhouse 4:30 A.M., arrived back at 11:00 A.M. . . . . This morning we did not ask any questions . . . and naturally followed the well-beaten trail . . . it looked less and less like the U.S. mail trail . . . a man with his dogs . . . told us we were 14 miles from Ophir . . . and would have to return there to get on the right trail . . . . Upon our arrival in Ophir I did not feel more tired than I would in going only a mile . . . . Left Ophir Roadhouse 12:30 P.M., arrived at Fritz's Roadhouse 9:50 P.M., 34 miles. Today I mushed 62 miles in 16 hours, 20 minutes."

April 16: "Left Fritz's Roadhouse 9:30 A.M., arrived at Halfway Roadhouse 6:45 P.M. 29 miles . . . . This Roadhouse was operated by . . . Shermier, who later figured in a U.S. Mail robbery that occurred at his roadhouse during the time that mail was hauled by dog teams."

April 17: "Left Shermier Roadhouse (Halfway Roadhouse) 11:00 A.M., arrived Iditarod 5:00 p.m., 16 miles."

S. Hall Young, pioneer Alaskan Presbyterian missionary, traveled

Landing from Steamer Corwin on ice edge, several miles from Nome. Dog teams used to haul people and supplies. Postcard, author's collection.

from Iditarod to Cordova in March 1912. He drove a team of five dogs 520 miles in 23 days to Seward where he boarded a steamer for Cordova.[8] He wrote of his trip:

"The beauty of 'dog mushing' is that you are compelled to work as hard as the dogs. You are not on a well-beaten boulevard; you are wending your way around trees and stumps, over hummocks, up and down hills, along the sides of mountains, and must keep your hands on the handle-bars, lifting the sled on the trail when it runs off and often breaking the trail ahead with your snowshoes.[9]

"We only made twenty miles the first day ... we are glad to stop at 'Bonanza Roadhouse' .... How good the moose meat tastes! How sweet the beds of hard boards and blankets! .... There is no floor in the roadhouse; all the lumber has been whipsawed by hand, the furniture manufactured out of boxes and stumps, the utensils of the rudest. But the luxury of splendid meat and good sour-dough bread and coffee makes us feel we have all that goes to make life desirable.[10]

"The longest distance we traveled in any one day was fifty-five miles; while our hardest and longest day's struggle through drifted snow and over a steep mountain yielded us only twelve miles of trail.[11]

"Not withstanding the heaviness of the trail, the bitter struggles over mountains and through deep snows .... I look back upon that trip and other trips like it with joyful recollections .... I would rather take a trip through that beautiful wilderness with my dogs, than travel luxuriously around the world in palatial steamboats. There is more fun in dog mushing."[12]

Hudson Stuck, Episcopal Archdeacon of the Yukon, also traveled the trail. In his book, *Ten Thousand Miles with a Dogsled*, he gives many vivid stories of travels along the trail. He notes that after crossing the Innoko the Kaltag trail is the trail to Nome.

"We reached it (the Yukon) again on the 23rd of March to Kaltag ... there was no narrow, dark line ... or even a faint, continuous inequality to hint that the trail had been .... The trail was wiped out and swallowed up by the late snows and winds."[13]

Enroute to Nikolai Stuck also had problems finding the trail.

"... I spied two stray dogs .... We followed the trail left by those dogs, growing fainter ... as the new snow fell .... We were four and a half hours making the eight miles or so to Nicoli's Village ... but might have been days making it but for those dogs."[14]

Goodwin, in his report of the 1908 Iditarod Trail Reconnaissance, gave vivid descriptions of his experiences also. After Kaltag the trail turned west and headed to the coast at Unalakleet.

"We arrived at Kaltag on March 19th, where we had the coldest weather of the entire trip ... 43 degrees below zero. Here we waited for telegrams, rested the dogs and arranged to go with the mail carriers as the weather was bad and trails obliterated.[15]

"On the 24th we made 40 miles to Unalaklik [sic] and this part especially needs attention ... many men have suffered hardships and have been lost in storms.[16]

"From Skaktoolik to Bonanza, 18 miles, the trail has been well staked.[16]

"... across Golovin Bay, the trail has been very well staked ... and has come in good stead as I am told by mail carriers that on every trip across Norton Bay they have had blizzards this winter."[17]

W.L. Goodwin reached Nome April 5, 1908 after a 66 day trip. He averaged 16.2 miles a day. Twelve days were lost to weather.

In 1910, by order of the Alaska Road Commission, the Iditarod Trail was blazed and surveyed by W.L. Goodwin with a crew of nine men and six teams of seven dogs each. They left Nome on November 9, 1910, and arrived in Seward on February 25, 1911. The men who established the Iditarod Trail were paid $3.50 a day, out of which 50¢ was taken each day for food. Besides surveying and blazing the trail, Goodwin was to locate sites for roadhouses. A log of distances was kept. Distances were measured by cyclometers attached to the sides of sleds. When the Alaska Railroad was completed in 1923, Nenana became the departure point for travelers headed for Iditarod and Nome.[18] That caused the Iditarod Trail to fall into disuse, except for small segments used for local travel.

In 1911 travelers were advised to purchase lots of rations at Susitna Station as it was the last store until Takotna, 238 miles away. In 1924 it cost $275 to travel from Anchorage to McGrath by dog team.[18] This high cost led many travelers to walk the trail as Charles Cadwallader did.

Nome beach and tent city, 1900. Postcard, author's collection.

Types of dogs and ships used by arctic explorers. Postcard, author's collection.

Nome Fire Dept., 1912, author's collection.

CHAPTER 2

Sled Dog Races Along the Iditarod Trail

This chapter provides a brief sampling of some of the races in communities along the Iditarod Trail during the years of its historic use as a winter trail. The second part contains a history of the current Iditarod Trail Sled Dog Race to Nome, including its beginning as a shorter race during the 1967 Alaska Purchase Centennial.

NOME AREA

The Nome Kennel Club was organized in 1908. Dog sled races were seen as not only providing winter entertainment, but also as a way of providing a consistent effort to improve the breed of sled dogs. Nome's major race, the All Alaska Sweepstakes, was held with much pomp and ceremony. Schools adjourned. The court adjourned. Most businesses closed. Green and gold pennants of the Nome Kennel Club fluttered everywhere. A fur-clad queen and her court rode in sleds drawn by powerful huskies. The racers waited in tense silence for the queen's flag to drop to signal the race start. They then sped forward along the 408 mile course from Nome on the Bering Sea to Candle on the Arctic Ocean and return.[1]

Messages were flashed constantly to the waiting hundreds. Detailed results were telegraphed and published in newspapers in many parts of the globe. Race rules dictated only one mandatory stop — at Candle, 204 miles from the starting point. Drivers could choose the length and location of the other stops. At those stops the dogs' needs were cared for first. They were rubbed down, fed, and bedded. Massages were provided to valued dogs whose legs had grown stiff.[1]

A team of Siberian huskies was entered in 1909 and attracted much attention. That summer Fox Ramsey traveled to Siberia and brought back a large number of these dogs and two individuals with experience in handling them. In 1910 he entered three teams of Siberians, and the popularity of the Siberian husky as a racer was established. (In the Nome race team owners often had others drive their teams, so one owner might have several teams in a race.)[1]

All Alaska Sweepstakes winners included: 1908 — John Hegness driv-

Crowd on Dog Race Day at Nome, Alaska. Dobbs photo postcard, author's collection.

ing Albert Fink's team; 1909 — "Scotty" Allan driving a J. Berger team; 1910 — John "Iron Man" Johnson driving a Col. Ramsey team; 1911-1912 — "Scotty" Allan driving the Allan and Darling team; 1913 — Fay Delzene driving the Bowen and Delzene team; 1914 — "Iron Man" Johnson, owner-driver; 1915-1916 — Leonhard Seppala, owner-driver. "Iron Man" Johnson's 1910 time of 74 hours, 14 minutes and 37 seconds has never been surpassed.[1]

On March 31, 1983, a 75th anniversary running of the Nome All Alaska Sweepstakes was held using the race rules of those early years. Rick Swenson won driving a team of his and Sonny Lindner's dogs.

Races were often run between Nome and Fort Davis bridge and return, a distance of over six miles. It was on this course that the Nome Kennel Club held its annual high school race, for both boys and girls. The ladies' race also used this route. Many impromptu contests used this popular trail[1].

After the major races of the season were over, and just before spring breakup made rivers and streams dangerous for travelers, a "joy race" was held. The Kamoogan handicap Burden Race went to Council, via Solomon, for a total of about 75 miles.[1]

Dog races were also held in nearby

LAWTON'S RACING TEAM, FIRST ANNUAL ALL-ALASKA SWEEPSTAKES, NOME, ALASKA.

RAMSAY WINNERS 2ND PRIZE 3RD ANNUAL ALL ALASKA SWEEPSTAKE NOME.

communities. The Solomon Derby was the second most popular racing event in the North. It was held in February. Due to its course being shorter than the Nome Sweepstakes Race speed was more important than the endurance qualities needed in the longer All Alaska Sweepstakes.[1]

FLAT AND IDITAROD

The first annual Iditarod Sweepstakes was held January 1, 1911, on a 20 mile course from Iditarod to Flat. The temperature was about zero, but high winds along some parts of the race trail reached near blizzard velocity. Claude Shea claimed the $350 first prize.[2]

The newly organized Iditarod Kennel Club held its first race on Thanksgiving, 1911. Late arrival of snow and poor trail conditions caused a trail course change from the original 15-mile course. Instead, a 2½ mile river loop was used. Prize money was raised at a masked ball a week earlier.[3]

On January 14, 1914, the first Ladies' Dog Team Race was held in the Flat-Iditarod area. Weather conditions were perfect with clear, calm weather just cold enough for good dog driving. Race bulletin boards were surrounded by eager, excited crowds. In Flat it appeared the entire populace turned out. The crowds gave as much applause and encouragement to those at the tail end as they did to front runners. The *Iditarod Pioneer* newspaper noted:

"The time made is remarkable, and is considerably below that of several races over the same course with men drivers, and only 20 minutes and 14 seconds higher than the record."[4]

Mrs. Swenson of Flat won with a time of 2 hours, 17 minutes and 58 seconds. Mrs. Crouse, also of Flat, came in second. Mrs. McGibney was third. There were six entrants. Mrs. Swenson drove a team of seven dogs. The other contestants had teams of five dogs. Mrs. Currin, who placed fourth, was cited for her "game" race as she maintained her position in spite of carrying one of her dogs in the sled for a great part of the race.[4,5]

RUBY AREA

Ruby had its own kennel club, and the annual Ruby Derby gained considerable fame. 1915 Nome All Alaska Sweepstakes winner Leonhard Seppala was invited to compete in the 1916 Ruby Derby. To participate he had to mush his team over 450 miles. The Ruby Derby was over a steep, rough trail from Ruby to Long City, a distance of 58 miles. Seppala won the race besting the 1913 record time by eight and a half minutes. Seppala's time was cut further in 1918 by George Jimmie, a Native. Jimmie had placed second in the 1916 race.[1,6]

One of the famous lead dogs in the Ruby Derby was Buster of Alec Brown's team. On his return from Long during one race he broke his leg at One Mile where the creek had glaciered up. He still finished the race, leading his team on three legs into Ruby. Buster was "pensioned off," later roaming Ruby streets at ease.[5,6]

Women competed in area races. An early consistent Kokrines Race winner was Alice Albert, grandmother of 1982 Iditarod finisher Rose Albert. Alice Albert loved racing so much she competed when she was dying of tuberculosis. She had to be placed in her sled, but her rapport with her team was such that they sped down the course with her seated in the sled. (Kokrines was 28 miles from Ruby.)[7]

Races in the mining areas continued until the decline in mining caused the population to dwindle. The dog sled races shifted to the Fairbanks area in the 1920s. Major races there have

Facing page, above: Lawton's racing team in the First Annual All-Alaska Sweepstakes, Nome, Alaska. B.B. Dobbs, photographer, Alaska Historical Library, Juneau. Below: Fox Ramsay, driver and owner, second prize winner, All-Alaska Sweepstakes, Nome, 1910. B.B. Dobbs, photographer, Alaska Historical Library.

This page, above: Alice Albert. Oil painting by her granddaughter, Rose Albert, from a photo taken when she was in her 20s. Right: Ladies Dog Race, Iditarod, 1914. William Ansley, photographer, Alaska Historical Library.

continued to the present with only a short break in the early 1940s.[8] In 1946 championship sled dog races in Anchorage were started during the February Fur Rendezvous.

When snowmobiles gained popularity in Alaska there was a decline in the number of dog teams in bush villages. Families no longer kept working dog teams. One of the goals of Joe Redington Sr. in developing the Iditarod Trail for an annual race was to bring back the dog teams in the villages.

THE IDITAROD TRAIL SLED DOG RACE

The annual Iditarod Trail Sled Dog Race to Nome came to life because of the hopes and dreams of Joe Redington Sr. and the Wasilla-Knik Centennial Committee. The Wasilla-Knik Centennial Committee, under chairperson Dorothy Page, was looking for a good project for the area celebration of the 100th anniversary of Alaska's purchase from Russia. They thought about having a race along the Iditarod Trail, but had difficulty interesting others about such a "folly."[7,9,10]

Dorothy Page ran into Joe and Vi Redington at the 1966 Willow Race, and asked what they thought of a race over the Iditarod Trail. The Redingtons agreed it was a fine idea, as they had been trying to promote interest in the old historic trail for years. Joe Redington said it had to be *big* for it to be successful, and suggested a $25,000 purse. Page was pleased to have found someone who was willing to help promote the idea of such a race and believed in it. She promptly appointed Joe and Vi to the Centennial Committee. They met with the Aurora Dog Mushers (which they were members of), and together the two organizations began the monumental task of putting on the first Iditarod Trail Race.[9;10]

Ed Carney donated countless hours with his HD-19 "Cat," eventually "burying" it in a swamp. Reynolds Equipment Company of Anchorage also donated use of their heavy equipment for trail work. Members of the Aurora Dog Mushers Club helped out, and the Iditarod Trail Leonhard Seppala Memorial Race took place in February 1967 with $25,000 in prize money.[10]

The $25,000 in prize money was raised by selling "Centennial Deeds" to a square foot of land on an acre at

Joe Redington Sr., "Father of the Iditarod," and Feets. Photo courtesy of Joe Redington Sr.

Flat Horn Lake, donated by the Redingtons from their homestead.[10]

The 1967 Iditarod Trail Seppala Memorial Race honored Leonhard Seppala, famous Nome racer, and the man who mushed the most miles (91) in the 1925 Diphtheria Serum Run. Fifty-eight mushers entered the race, including two women: Shirley Gavin and Gloria Jones. Fifty-four mushers finished. Held on February 11th and 12th, it covered over 28 miles of trail each day. Temperatures hovered around zero, and trail conditions were less than ideal. Issac Okleasik of Teller, victor in the Willow Winter Carnival Sled Dog Race one week earlier, won the race. His total elapsed time of 3 hours, 50 minutes, and 53 seconds was more than two minutes faster than second place finisher Pete Shepard of Fairbanks. Shirley Gavin placed 27th in the race. Gloria Jones dropped out after losing her dogs the first day of the race.[11;12;13]

The 1968 Iditarod Trail Race was cancelled due to lack of snow. Noted sprint racer George Attla, the "Huslia Hustler," came in first in 1969. There were no Iditarod Trail races in 1970, 1971, and 1972. However, Joe Redington Sr. continued to push for prize money for the race. It was Redington who kept hopes for the race alive and was instrumental in securing the support to extend the race trail to Nome.[10;14]

Sled Dog Races in Ruby, Alaska. The Anchorage Museum.

Howard Farley of Nome was enlisted to work at developing the trail from the northern end. In 1972 the U.S. Army combined cold weather maneuvers with locating and marking the Iditarod Trail. Joe Redington Sr. and Dave Olson of Knik began working along with about 50 army personnel in April. Intensive efforts were made to mark the trail from Susitna Station to McGrath with old style tripod markers, such as originally were spaced along the Iditarod Trail.[10;15]

After two weeks of hard work, the last Sunday in April was set aside for an Iditarod Trail "winter carnival" including a sled dog race. On Monday, April 25th, Lt. Gen. Ruegg visited the Iditarod Trail Headquarters, and skied along part of the reopened trail. He then participated in a sled dog race against Brigade Commander Col. Bender, and won by 43 seconds.[15]

THE IDITAROD SLED DOG RACE TO NOME

1973 marks the beginning of the current Iditarod Trail Race from Anchorage to Nome. Thirty-four mushers started the race. Twenty-two completed the 1,100 mile journey to Nome. Dick Wilmarth of Red Devil, Alaska, had a winning time of 20 days, 49 minutes and 41 seconds. He was awarded $12,000. Twelve days later the last musher, John Schultz of Delta Junction, pulled into Nome closing the books on the first Iditarod race to go over most segments of the trail.

The 1974 race saw the first female entrants in the race between Anchorage and Nome. Mary Shields and Lolly Medley, both from the Fairbanks area, finished 23rd and 24th, proving that women could indeed complete the race. Skeptics who did not believe a woman could travel without help along the trail had to deal with the fact that Shields, a few days after the race, turned around and mushed alone along the trail to Galena. There spring breakup made her stop and fly the rest of the way home. Carl Huntington of Galena was the 1974 race winner.

The 1975 race winner was Emmitt Peters of Ruby, Alaska. Only one female, Ginger Burcham of Tok, Alaska, entered that year. She scratched at Finger Lake checkpoint.

There were no female entrants in 1976. Jerry Riley of Nenana, Alaska, won the race that year.

In 1977 two females entered the race. Varona Thompson placed 34th. Minnesota entrant Dinah Knight scratched at Iditarod checkpoint. Rick Swenson of Eureka, Alaska, won the 1977 race.

Susan Butcher, Shelley (Vandiver) Gill, and Varona Thompson entered the race in 1978. For the first time women placed "in the money" as Butcher and Thompson finished 19th and 20th respectively. Dick Mackey of Wasilla, Alaska, won the race. ("In the money" refers to placing in the positions where money is awarded. Since 1973 money has been awarded to the top 20 finishers except in 1975 when money only went to the top 15.)

In 1979 both female entrants finished in the money. Susan Butcher became the first female to place in the top ten, finishing 9th. Patty Friend came in 20th. Rick Swenson came in first, becoming the first musher to win the race twice. From 1978 on at least one female has finished in the money in every Iditarod race!

1980 saw seven women enter the race. Two placed in the top 10 — Susan Butcher in 5th position and Donna Gentry in 10th position. Donna was "rookie of the year" that year. Libby Riddles, in her first Iditarod, also finished in the money in 18th place. Dee Dee Jonrowe, Marjorie Ann Moore, and Barbara Moore also completed the race. Joe May was the 1980 race champion.

In 1981 three women again placed in the money with Susan Butcher again in 5th position, Donna Gentry in 18th place, and Libby Riddles in 20th position. Dee Dee Jonrowe and Sue Firmin placed 31st and 32nd of

Above, 1974 U.S. Post Office cachet.

Below, 1983 Nome Kennel Club cachet. Racers carry similar cachets each year.

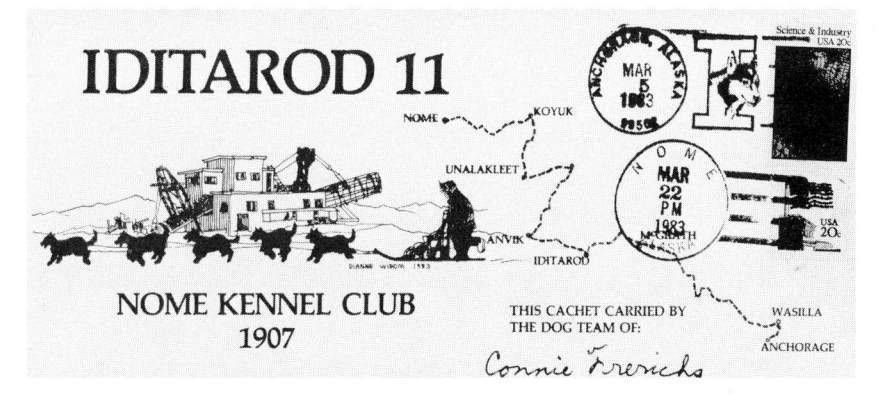

13

the 53 entrants. Rick Swenson won the race for an unprecedented third time.

1982 was a superb year for Susan Butcher. She placed 2nd, only 3 minutes and 43 seconds behind race winner Rick Swenson. A consistent top finisher, Butcher was now being seen as a serious contender for winning the race. Rose Albert finished 32nd of the 54 entrants. Rick Swenson was now a four-time winner, winning for the second year in a row.

1983 saw ten women enter the race, the largest number to date. Nine finished the race. Susan Butcher, Susan Firmin, and Dee Dee Jonrowe all placed in the money in 9th, 14th and 15th positions respectively. Rick Mackey won, making the first father-son winning combination. His father, Dick Mackey had won in 1978.

In 1984 nine women entered the race. Susan Butcher again placed second. Dean Osmar of Clam Gulch, Alaska was an unexpected winner. In 1984 Kari Skogan of Norway became the first woman from a foreign nation to enter the race. She finished in 35th place.

Five women entered the race in 1985. Top contender Susan Butcher was forced to drop out of the race when a moose attacked her team killing two of her dogs and injuring most of the rest of her team. Libby Riddles surprised many people when she kept the lead by driving out of Shaktoolik into a howling storm. That daring gamble paid off. Libby Riddles became the first woman to win the Iditarod Race. LIBBY WINS! was triumphantly repeated across the state and nation, and the Iditarod race commanded an even greater share of national and world media attention than ever before.

In 1985 three French mushers entered the Iditarod Race: a husband and wife team Claire and Jacques Philip, and Monique Bene. The largest contingent from any foreign nation to compete, they were three of the eight mushers from foreign nations in 1985. Mushers from Australia, Germany, Great Britain, Italy and Japan also competed.

An interesting sidelight on Alaska's relationship with dog sled teams and France is the part dog teams played in the mountains of France during World War I. In 1914, Rene Haas of the French Army, a Nome resident when the war broke out, convinced his government of the potential of dog sled teams. Haas returned to Alaska after engaging the famous Nome musher Scotty Allan to help him obtain dogs for service in France.[16]

> "Then came the day, filled with excitement and thrills, when on a tow-line three hundred and fifty feet long, one hundred and six famous dogs passed through the streets of the far-away Alaska town, on their way to the battlefields of France."[17]

Scotty Allan, a famous Nome All Alaska Sweepstakes Race winner, had the job of training the young chasseurs ("Blue Devils") to handle the dogs. He taught them simple commands such as "Gee," "Haw," "Whoa," and "Mush." The dog teams' first feat was to carry 90 tons of ammunition to a French battery that had been cut off from supplies and was out of shells and bullets. Horses and mules had tried for two weeks to reach the soldiers without success. The dogs reached the isolated French battery within four days. Another group of dogs strung over twenty miles of telephone wire in a single night, establishing communication with a different detachment that had been cut off by the Germans.[18]

IDITAROD MUSHERS CARRY THE MAIL

In 1974, the second year of the race to Nome, the U.S. Post Office prepared cacheted envelopes for race entrants to carry over the trail during the race. These cachets commemorated the historic role of the mail carrier who carried mail by dog team over the trail in the early years of this century. In an advertisement headlined "Mushers Reenact an Era" the post office stated:

> "This will be the first official dog team mail contract in twenty-five years. The mushers in the 1974 Iditarod Race will carry these specially printed envelopes all 1,049 miles from Anchorage to Nome. All cachets will be cancelled in Anchorage prior to departing on the historic mail route and backstamped upon arrival in Nome."[19]

The U.S. Post Office did not continue the practice for the 1975 race. In 1975 the Nome Kennel Club designed a special envelope for the race, and has continued having cacheted envelopes carried each year. These cachets are part of the official required gear that each musher carries and must show to official race checkers at each checkpoint along the trail.

Photographers lined up at 1983 Iditarod Race, Anchorage starting line. R. Nielsen photo.

CHAPTER 3

Women in the Iditarod Race: The Pioneers 1974-1977

The first women to participate in the Anchorage to Nome Iditarod Trail Race ran in 1974. Mary Shields and Lolly Medley, both from the Fairbanks area, signed up the second year the race went to Nome. Shields and Medley did not know each other prior to the race, but enroute to Nome, traveling separately, they kept seeing each other and became acquainted. Both mushed their teams across Nome's finish line to the surprise of some individuals who felt women could not tolerate the rigors of the trail.

Ginger Burcham, then of Tok, Alaska, paid her entry fee for the 1975 race to Nome. Starting with a team of Samoyeds, she ended up scratching from the race after encountering deep snows in Rainy Pass. No women entered the 1976 race.

In 1977 Varona Thompson and Dinah Knight entered the Iditarod. Knight was the first woman from outside the state of Alaska to compete in the race, but did not make it to the Nome finish line. Thompson finished the race in 34th position.

This chapter and the following chapters contain brief sketches or profiles of all the women who have run the Iditarod race to date. These mushers are placed in chapters relative to the first year they ran in the race. Each one's place in the chapter is in the order in which she finished that first year she raced. Unless otherwise footnoted all quotations in the text came from interviews, conversations, and correspondence with each musher. All 29 women have been contacted by this writer, and have had an opportunity to provide information for this book as well as respond to the material to ensure as much as possible accuracy of facts related herein.

MARY SHIELDS

Mary Shields, an enthusiastic, energetic, ruddy faced Alaskan has the honor of being the first female to mush across the finish line at Nome in the Iditarod Trail Sled Dog Race, having placed 23rd in the 1974 race.

Her pioneering race experience came a few short years after spending her first Alaskan winter alone in an old cabin at the base of Chulitna Butte, 13 miles from the nearest community at Gold Creek. That October some friends offered to loan her their old freight sled and three sled dogs for her use in hauling water and firewood. From this loan an abiding love for dog team travel and exploring the winter countryside grew.

"Over the winter, the country taught me many lessons. Being by myself, I had time to watch and listen. I heard the

Mary Shields. Photo by Evelyn Trabent; courtesy of the Fairbanks Daily News Miner.

singing of my own heart — the joys, the fears, the questions, the unanswerables. A peace filled me and gave me strength I had not known before."[1]

Cabbage, Mary's lead dog, was one of six pups born to Kiana, leader of that borrowed sled dog team. Given by Mary to the rangers at the then-McKinley Park, he was returned to her as his black lab heritage detracted from the husky appearance that park visitors expected to see. Cabbage then became Mary's first sled dog of her own and the nucleus of her Iditarod team.

On March 4, 1974, the 38th starting position in the second Iditarod race was occupied by Mary and her team of eight dogs — the smallest team competing in the race. Six were veteran dogs of hers who had accompanied her on a number of trips and two were new recruits. Within the first hour of her departure the remaining five teams passed her.

The second race night was spent in a tent near Ptarmigan Pass with several mushers including the other female racer, Lolly Medley.

She describes waking up to a frightening scene:

> ". . . not a nose, ear or tip of a tail could be seen where the night before four dog teams had been standing. I went over to where my team should have been and found eight little steam geysers vented up through small blowholes in the wind-packed snow. I dug with a panicked heart, and just below the surface there was a cozy, black Cabbage, snug in his nest but happy to see me . . . . I moved along the blowholes. All the dogs were alive . . . ."[2]

A few days later at McGrath she took her 24-hour, compulsory layover. There she dropped Thunder, one of her two new recruits, as she was tired of nagging him and he had never pulled his full share. The rest of her dogs were in good shape, except for Ambler whose left front foot pad was raw. Along with dog booties and antibiotics from the veterinarian Ambler continued on to Nome.

When she pulled into Shaktoolik, several teams pulled out. The checker explained, laughing, that the men had planned to stay the night, but when they saw her coming they hurriedly harnessed up their tired dog teams as they didn't want to be passed by a woman!

Along about Elim, Mary's competitiveness overtook her and she decided she wanted to be the first female to reach Nome. Her competitor, Lolly Medley, was traveling slower but rested less. The two kept seeing each other. At Solomon, the last checkpoint before Nome, Lolly arrived a couple hours later than Mary. She and Mary decided to rest. When Mary awoke a few hours later Lolly was already on the trail for Nome.

Mary then began a chase. She mushed on for miles, but could not see Lolly's headlamp. There were only ten miles left. Then the dogs bunched up, confused about the trail. Lights were moving along the road to the right, and Mary felt they were Lolly's escort, about a mile ahead. She veered down to the beach ice and ran behind her team to lighten their load and increase speed. But she couldn't catch up. So she headed to the road and surprised some race fans who, listening to their radio, knew Lolly had left first. They assumed Mary was Lolly, as they had noticed a headlight further down the trail. Delighted by this news, Mary headed down the ice again and a little later arrived on Front Street, Nome.

Crossing the finish line with seven of the eight dogs she started with 28 days earlier, she was welcomed with a thundering reception from the crowd. About 30 women in parkas and kuspuks held a banner over their heads across the finish line saying "You've Come a Long Way, Baby."[3] Lolly came in 26 minutes later.

Nome treated Mary and Lolly well, giving them the fanciest suite at the Nome Inn with baskets of fresh fruit on the dresser, fresh flowers and champagne. Appreciated even more was a "steamy deep tub"[4] and clean sheets. The next night the second mushers' banquet was held. After two days Mary headed home.

Instead of a plane ride home to Fairbanks, Mary started mushing her dogs back along the Iditarod Trail. Without the pressure of the race she was able to enjoy the splendor of the scenery and visit friends. Traveling up the Yukon by night to take advantage of the cooler temperatures when the trail hardened up after the day's thaw, she was able to enjoy the warm daytime sunshine while she napped. She found many villages were holding their spring carnivals, and the heavy traffic up and down the river packed the trail like a highway. On April 15th, two weeks after leaving Nome, Mary reached Galena, about 500 miles away. The snows were rapidly melting. Breakup was coming fast. To avoid the expense of chartering a plane further down the trail, Mary decided to fly from Galena. She tried to hitch a ride on an empty military plane at the Air Base, but to no avail. Fortunately Wien Airlines was agreeable to taking her at the special musher's rate. But the agent interpreted the rules to mean she had to have a cage for each dog, the purchase of which would raise the cost dramatically. By chance a Galena resident overheard her problem, and offered her the loan of his son's dog box. The offer was gratefully accepted. Mary's dogs rode home in Carl Huntington's (the 1974 Iditarod race winner) dog crate. And Mary said good-bye to the greatest adventure of her life up till that time.

Mary's adventures continue each winter. In 1984 her book, *Sled Dog Trails,* was published. That same year she was one of 26 mushers to compete in the first Yukon Quest International Sled Dog race, traveling over 1,000 miles from Fairbanks, Alaska, to Whitehorse, Yukon Territory. She placed 16th of the 20 finishers.

Mary Shields divides her time between her winter cabin at Schmmelpfenning Creek, Alaska, about 35 miles west of Fairbanks, and a summer back road cabin near Fairbanks. She works as a seasonal fish and game technician, and is a free lance writer. During the summer of 1985 she gave sled dog demonstrations to passengers taking a riverboat tour of the Fairbanks area. During the winters she has traveled thousands of miles by dog sled with her husband, John Manthei.

Since her arrival as a 20-year-old Campfire Girls counselor in 1965, she has found a way of life that combines the best of Alaska's heritage and promise. Mary Shields personifies the best of the tradition of the pioneering spirit found in Alaskans.

LOLLY MEDLEY

Lolly Medley was one of two female mushers in the 1974 Iditarod race. Always interested in dogs, her first experience with using sleds with dogs came at age 12. She made a harness for her long-haired German Shepherd and had her pull a toboggan up a hill. Then she'd turn the dog loose, ride the toboggan down hill, and start the process all over.

While serving as a VISTA volunteer in Vermont in 1964-65, she decided to get a dog. She heard of a woman in Swanton, Vermont, who raised sled dogs. She was introduced to registered Siberian Huskies when she visited Dolly Seamore. Seamore informed her that malamutes were too slow. Medley was impressed by the Siberians' friendliness and attitude, and soon brought home two Siberians. When she left Vermont she had five or six registered Siberians. She returned to college studies, interspersed with working to support herself. In 1970 she graduated from Chico State College in California with a degree in child development and nutrition. Soon she headed for Alaska.

In 1972-73 she helped Bud Smyth train his 1974 Iditarod race team. At the last minute it was apparent there were enough dogs for two teams. She decided not to be a last minute entrant in the 1973 race due to a lack of food ready for the necessary food drops to checkpoints and other logistical problems.

She started the 1974 Iditarod with 14 dogs and finished with 9 dogs. Lots of the race was enjoyable. However, a couple of times she became discouraged and hoped that "a helicopter would land so I could drive my team on." Her discouragement lifted after she solved her emergency, prior to arriving at the next checkpoint. By then she determined to continue in the race.

Reflecting on the 1974 race she comments that it was a lot less sophisticated. The equipment is much different today. Then all racers used

Lolly Medley at 1984 race start. Jim Brown photo.

heavy canvass tarps lashed in their sleds to hold their equipment. The first regular use of sled bags didn't come until the 1976 race. The canvass tarps were never tied the same way twice. In 1973 some racers did not use padded harnesses. The 1974 rules called for padded ones. In contrast to sprint racing, where padding was unnecessary, Iditarod racers discovered the dog's fur was rubbed off without padding to protect it over long distances.

She remembers the best part of the 1974 and 1984 Iditarod races that she ran as the people she met along the trail. She felt the villagers treated her "like a member of the family." It was a real thrill to be around them as they gave so much of themselves. She finished in 24th position in 1974. Heading into Nome she was ahead of Mary Shields. Lolly received bad directions and went over a mountain outside of Nome. Mary had gone over sea ice. When she got to Nome she found Mary had arrived about 30 minutes earlier. "It was really cute. Neither of us knew where the other was." Both were warmly greeted by everyone there. They received roses and lots of gifts from residents of Nome. It was a "real tearjerker" and made her feel that everybody was on her side.

In 1984 Lolly decided to run on the 10th anniversary of her first Iditarod. Her experience was quite different. Her team was much faster. In 1974 her team went about five miles per hour. In 1984 her team trotted at 15 miles per hour. Halfway between Rohn River and Nikolai she ran into a stump, jammed her knee on the back stanchion of her sled, and broke her knee. After flying back to Palmer for medical attention, she continued in the race. When she reached Ruby, some of her dogs were getting sick so she scratched. Her main leaders in 1984 were her old dog Gypsy, Happy, and two young speedsters, Cookie and Foxie. Gypsy really enjoyed the race, gaining 10 pounds by the time she reached Ruby. When Medley really wanted to make time she moved Cookie and Foxie into double lead.

In 1976 Lolly instituted the Golden Harness award for a special dog in the race. During that race she flew along the trail, covering the race as a reporter for the *Fairbanks News Miner*. When she flew back to Fairbanks for a brief stop she sewed up several gifts for mushers. One was a harness inscribed with "1974 Iditarod" and "Piper," Ken Chase's lead dog's name. The Golden Harness award is now important to the mushers, and it means a lot to the ones who have won it. Now the mushers themselves vote on the winner. Lolly feels every dog in the race deserves an award. That is the basis of the Golden Harness.

Lolly Medley now runs a harness shop and sells a number of things to sled dog enthusiasts. She began making her own harnesses in 1970. She got tired of going to the store and buying collars that didn't last so she started making her own. Her first harnesses were hand made and sewn with dental floss. Very quickly people started asking her to make them some. Most of the time she has worked out of her own home. In recent years she has begun making sled bags. She made her first one for Dick Mackey's 1978 race. It took her nearly two months of looking at the sled and material he brought her before she designed a pattern and began working on it. Noting that 1985 has been a year of many sled bag orders, she says it takes three full days to cut one out and sew it.

Lolly Medley is a very busy person. She is raising three children. Her oldest, Ramie, age 10, was born the same day that Emmitt Peters won the 1975 Iditarod, coming into the world a few hours before Peters' entrance on Nome's Front Street. Laura was born in 1979. Shelly was only 15 months old when her mother entered the 1984 Iditarod. Raising and supporting her family alone while training for the race, Lolly notes that dog training sessions often took place between midnight and 3:00 a.m.

The daughter of a truck driver and a registered nurse, she moved frequently as a youngster. She estimates she attended 12 or 13 schools before graduating from high school. It made her an expert in adjusting to new situations. She feels she received a much broader education because of moving around and coming in contact with lots of different kinds of people.

She has run in the Women's World Championships in Anchorage, the open World Championships in Anchorage, and the Women's North American race in Fairbanks. She notes that you train completely differently for the shorter races. She personally feels that the Iditarod is easier on the dogs than the shorter races. There is not the pressure on the dogs. Although there are a lot more miles she feels they are easier miles for the dogs, not the musher.

Lolly feels that her VISTA service has been a major influence on her. She feels it is the most fascinating thing she has done in her life. She became more aware of herself as a person. The harder she worked, the more she learned. It was quite an "eye opener." She feels she was given, mentally, much more than she could ever possibly return. She was trained to test for and teach children and adults in remedial reading. However, actual duties ranged from transporting people to medical appointments, help with homemaking, and doing whatever was needed. She was very impressed by the people — their openness, their friendliness, and the love they showed; and their willingness to help her and her fellow volunteers. She learned what poverty is. She learned to be able to appreciate what she has. She feels her basic needs are met now. She doesn't need anything else. This enables her to give — to give and not feel resentful that something is taken from her.

This attitude of giving and sharing is expressed in her daily relationships with people. She openly shares of herself with others. Her spirit of openness and sharing is one that is so important. It is why the mushers recall their experiences in the villages so positively. The villagers share openly in the same ways Vermonters shared with her.

Although she is not running the Iditarod in 1986, she plans to run it again. She keeps adding to her dog lot. Now numbering between 60 and 70, it has been as high as 300 in the past. She continues helping mushers in her own unique ways, giving advice, answering questions, and doing what she can to share her knowledge and concern for others.

GINGER BURCHAM

Ginger Burcham, then of Tok, Alaska, was the third female to enter the Iditarod race. She started with a team of ten Samoyed and Samoyed-Siberian crosses in 1975. Due to last minute problems she needed to use several puppies in her team. One dog had only a few miles of training. She ended up scratching from the race at Finger Lake after becoming exhausted searching for the trail through Ptarmigan Pass on snowshoes ahead of her team in five feet of snow. Her dogs were still ready to run when she scratched.

Reflecting on her experience Burcham states: "I was very ill prepared for the race." Only four of her dogs were well trained. Her lead dog, Goldy, was a trail leader. As long as she could see the trail she was fine. She was not able to smell out a trail, however. Goldy, a female, came into season the day before the race, complicating her problems.

Ginger Burcham and Apollo. Photo courtesy of Ginger Burcham.

Due to illness she was not able to come to Anchorage until a couple of days before the race. The dogs did not have time to adjust to the change, and had problems with illness. All had diarrhea at first, causing her to stop every few hours. By the third day of the race they started feeling better. They were running well.

When she came to Ptarmigan Pass she was behind Norman Vaughan's team. There were several teams behind her. Vaughan had gone ahead of her. A blizzard had blown out the trail. There were markers about every 100 yards. You could not see from one marker to the next one. Going ahead on snowshoes, looking for the trail, she became exhausted. Her dogs had no experience following her. She had to drag them to get them going. After five hours, she decided it was best to turn around and scratch. She feels if her team had been more experienced she probably would have done okay. The dogs were still ready to go when she quit. It was Burcham who was afraid she couldn't find the trail over the pass.

A decade later she says, "I loved it. I had a ball out there." She would love to run it again. She has a better team now than she had then. She is aware of many of the mistakes she made in her preparations. She had trained on flat land. Yet the first part of the race was up and down hills. She and the dogs didn't know anything about hills. Her sled had over 200 pounds of gear. Her food had not gotten out to the checkpoints, so she was carrying her own food for the entire race on the sled. Her snowshoes were too big. A lot of her gear was the wrong stuff.

She had small dogs for that era. Some of her dogs weighed as little as 35 pounds. Others were 45 pounds. Her original team contained six Samoyeds: Tok (a leader), Buck, Shukan, Pearl, Rama and Voka; plus three Samoyed and Siberian crosses: Rondy, Trusty and Goldy (her main leader). She had one "Black Alaskan," Black Joe, who was dropped because of bad feet. Pearl was replaced by Nicki after a training accident. Training runs started with four miles a day. They were increased to 30 miles or more at the time before the race. Training temperatures were mostly below zero degrees, and dropped as low as -45 degrees.

About a year after the race, Ginger and her family moved to Virginia to be closer to her husband's parents as his mother was quite ill. She has continued her interest in dogs and in Samoyeds. She is a charter member of the Organization for the Working Samoyed. She runs sled dog demonstrations during the Christmas season. Impressed with the Samoyed, she feels they make excellent family dogs. She continues to race her team. She has raised all the dogs she runs, and breeds them for working dogs. She also shows them. One, Lace, wins just about every time he is shown.

Her hobbies include painting. She sells most of her artwork, and specializes in acrylics and pastels. She likes to sew and knit. She was attending college taking computer programmer courses in the fall of 1985. She and her husband live in a 200-year-old colonial home which they are restoring.

Ginger is one of three daughters of Wally and Angeline Brown. She spent most of her childhood in Alaska. Many years were spent in Eagle, Alaska, and in the Tok area. At age 13 she had her first dog team. When she was 16 her family left Alaska. After her marriage to Richard Burcham she returned to Alaska. Her interest in sled dog racing was sparked by helping her sister, Susan Martinique, train a team. She fell in love with the Samoyed breed when she saw a beautiful Samoyed team running on a lake. She was unable to find any Samoyeds in Alaska so she had them shipped from Seattle to get her team started.

Ginger was active as a sprint racer in the Tok area. She was Limited Class champion the first year they had the Limited Class. Her neighbor, Bill Arpino, ran the Iditarod in 1973, finishing in 11th position. His experience sparked her interest in the Iditarod. Arpino built her a light freight sled for her Iditarod race. She is still interested in the Iditarod, and hopes that one day she will again take to the trail in a future Iditarod race.

At present she keeps busy with her college studies, her hobbies, and raising her family. Her two daughters, Lorraina and Doriena, are in college. Her son, Robert, is in high school.

VARONA THOMPSON

Varona Thompson, the third female musher to cross the finish line of an Iditarod race, has the distinction of being the first woman to run the race twice. She is the second woman to place in the money. Her 20th place finish in the 1978 race netted her $500.

Her introduction to the race came through her father. Larry Thompson was an Iditarod volunteer pilot who delivered food to checkpoints and flew along the trail during the early years of the race. Varona's decision to enter the Iditarod came out of youthful determination and spunk in reaction to someone telling her she couldn't make it to Nome. At age 22 she was visiting her father in Kaltag after returning from an extended vacation stateside. Reminiscing about that decision she recalls:

"I was looking out the window at his (Richard Burnham's) dogs out in the yard. And I said, 'That's what I should do. I should run the race.' And this guy, his name is Austin, told me that I couldn't do it. And he said . . . 'You're a woman.' I said, 'I bet ya I could.' He says, 'Naw. You can't do it.' I says, 'I'm gonna.'

". . . (we) went to Anchorage. Bought some dogs out of these people's back yards . . . . I got a couple of dogs from Libby Riddles. And the most expensive dog I had cost $25.00 A real bargain! . . . . I got one dog from the pound, and he turned out to be my best one. He ended up being the leader."

She trained for about four months before her first Iditarod race in 1977. Her dad's business partner had run the Iditarod earlier. He was also training and gave her a few pointers. There were many other things she wished she had known about before her first Iditarod race. Paramount among them was foot problems. Prior to the race she had not experienced foot problems with her dogs.

"When I got out on the trail my dogs were dropping off like flies . . . . I dropped a lot of dogs because of feet even

Varona Thompson.

though I didn't know why they didn't want to run anymore. By the time I actually found out what was wrong I'd already dropped half my team only three checkpoints out (from the start) . . ."

Part of the difficulty in determining what their problems were was that the dogs' feet weren't cut. They were just sore.

She remembers the best part of the race as meeting the other mushers. For the first three days she traveled by herself. When she pulled into Rohn River there were lots of folks there. At one point the mushers gathered around her. They sang "Happy Birthday" to mark her 23rd birthday. Having caught up with the group she continued to travel with Bud Smyth. He ran that year wearing a face mask and claiming he was Vasily Zamitykn of Ayak Island, Russia. She describes him as the "trail sweeper" who kept the other tail end mushers going. Vasily won the Red Lantern award for finishing last. She placed 34th.

Looking at her three race experiences (1977, 1978 and 1980), she remembers the first race as the most fun. "There was more pressure the second time." Describing her 1977 team as "a five-mile-per-hour team," her 1978 team was much speedier. It could go 10 to 13 miles per hour. For the 1978 race she was training in the Goose Bay area with Dick Mackey. She was his dog handler. In the 1977 race she finished five days behind the leaders. In 1978 she made it to Nome less than two days behind Dick Mackey, who won by one second over Rick Swenson. Her 1978 dogs were Mackey's second team, composed primarily of young dogs under two years old. Her lead dog, Penny, had run with Dick Mackey for seven years. Varona feels Penny was burned out on running and being leader.

During her first race she had problems feeding her dogs. Her honeyballs were made up of dry dog food and peanut butter and honey. The dogs wouldn't eat them. She also had salmon heads which she hadn't precooked. She had to cook them on the trail. She had not taken a Coleman stove as people told her it was too heavy. She finally was able to obtain one when she reached Rohn River. By then she had lost valuable time trying to keep a campfire going. Her dogs wouldn't eat the food she had prepared for them. Fortunately she was able to obtain some other food. Her dogs had been trained with dry fish and lots of water. The food that she took for their race was quite different than their training diet. That accentuated their eating problems.

She trained in the Kaltag area. During the Iditarod race, when she reached the training turnaround point on the race trail her dogs wanted to go back home.

Thompson states that if she were competing in the race today, with the experience she had prior to the 1977 race, it is unlikely she would have made it to Nome.

Her 1977 race problems and mistakes were carefully analyzed. She learned from them. The next year she and Dick Mackey made two main burners on her stove. She precooked all her dog food. She also had more variety. Her personal food was never very good, in her opinion. She took quick food. The first year it was mainly beef jerky, chocolate bars and other "junk food" that didn't need cooking. Hot meals were obtained at checkpoints. "The bad thing about eating at checkpoints is that it made you tired."

She had no intention of competing in the 1978 Iditarod. She was working for Dick Mackey, helping him train his team. He came in one day and told her she had a sponsor. Rosemary Phillips of Nome had paid her entry fee. That was the beginning of a long association with Phillips, who has been one of the mainstays of the Iditarod race in its early years.

Looking back on her second race experience, Thompson recalls:

"It was kind of neat. I helped train the team that won it that year. Even though it was by a second . . . he won!

"That was the first year I ran with Susan Butcher. All through that year when we were training she was training out in Goose Bay too. They were saying how tough she was. So I felt like I was competing in probably two categories . . . .

"I was just really excited to have a team that actually ran . . . . I had really young dogs . . . . You kind of had to baby them . . . . You didn't want to burn them out so bad that they aren't going to be any good the next year. You don't want them to hate running anymore, so you really had to look at their attitude."

After the 1978 race she acquired another dog team. The dogs were fighters. The team was unmanageable. Eventually she ended up buying more dogs, mainly from the Nome area. She took off a year before entering the 1980 Iditarod. Only half of the team in the 1980 race was the team she purchased in 1978. During the race there were constant dog fights. She was not able to obtain needed rest. "It was a bad year altogether." She ended up scratching from the race. She has not entered the Iditarod again.

Varona Thompson is no longer mushing dogs. In the fall of 1985 she was a student at Alaska Vocational College. Prior to moving to the Wasilla area she lived a number of years in Nome. There she first worked for sponsor Rosemary Phillips at the Nome Liquor Store. Later she worked as a dental assistant in Nome for one-and-a-half years. Still not settled into her ultimate career goals, she feels she would like to own her own business.

Born in Arizona, Varona Thompson came to Alaska at age 6. She grew up in Anchorage where she graduated from high school. As a youngster she hated cold weather. When her family moved to a better insulated home her attitude changed. She found it was the poorly insulated home that contributed to her always feeling cold before. Now she likes Alaska and plans to remain here. The oldest of four children, she currently resides in the Wasilla area.

Today Varona Thompson can

look back on her Iditarod experiences and see she was an inspiration as well as a pioneer. As a female she wasn't initially taken seriously. Yet her dogged determination kept her involved. Although she has no future plans to compete again, she set the stage for women being seen as repeat mushers in the race. As mushers they do compete on equal footing with men as a person's sex is no barrier when a person trains seriously and learns from their experiences.

DINAH KNIGHT

Dinah Knight of Minneapolis, Minnesota, entered the 1977 Iditarod race. She was the first woman from outside of Alaska to enter the Iditarod. Knight had raced the Minnesota and Wisconsin dog sled race circuit for a number of years before coming to Alaska for the Iditarod race. In retrospect she feels she should have spent the entire winter in Alaska to better prepare herself for Alaskan conditions. Encountering a number of unexpected problems, she was forced to scratch at the Iditarod checkpoint.

Now Dinah Ellingson, of Richfield, Minnesota, she became interested in sled dog racing while attending the Minnesota Winter Carnival. There she "fell in love with dog sled racing." She acquired a five-dog team and began to race. When she read about the 1973 Iditarod race it seemed to be "the ultimate" and a superb challenge. Now she states respectfully, "I didn't realize it was as big an experience as it was."

She obtained more dogs and for four years prepared to run the Iditarod. An outdoors adventure-oriented person, she feels she was ill prepared for the toughness of the race — the "morning and nights of racing." She feels no matter how much you train in Minnesota you are not prepared for Alaska conditions. Minnesota is

Dinah Knight at vet check. From 1978 **Iditarod Annual**. *Rosemary Phillips photograph.*

quite flat in comparison to the hills and mountains of the Iditarod Trail. She had no awareness of how rough Alaska storms could be. Reflecting back on her experience, she feels that anyone from outside Alaska should come to Alaska and spend two or three winters familiarizing themselves with Alaska conditions.

Prior to the race she had not really known anyone who had raced in the race. (Only four previous entrants came from outside of Alaska.) She feels she knew very little about the race itself. "If I knew then what I know now about the race, I wouldn't run it."

Mixed in with the less pleasant memories of the race are memories of Alaskans as "helpful, welcoming and hospitable." She was deeply impressed by the hospitality of Alaskans. No matter what time of day or night you arrived, they always had something hot for you to eat — such as moose stew. They were ready for you at all hours, around the clock. She feels she wasn't able to do one tenth enough to repay their kindness.

She has worked with dogs all her life. When she started the race she felt strongly about wanting to finish with all her dogs. (She had flown her team from Minnesota to Anchorage for the race.) She feels one needs to know when to drop dogs and when to keep them so one is able to collect their dropped dogs. She feels her lack of experience affected her in that she should have pushed a lot harder than she did.

Several nights into the race she had an accident. Her sled hit a tree. The dogs ran away with her sled. She finally caught up with them further down the trail. One of her dogs was badly injured when twisted by one of the lines. This accident unnerved her. It caused her to fall back in the pack and lose considerable time. A storm wiped out the trail. She was far behind. Talking things over, she decided to scratch at Iditarod.

Looking back on the race she has lots of painful memories. She got out of sled dog racing. But she has never quit her involvement with dogs. She now has coursing dogs and travels extensively around the United States to participate in field trials.

A native of New York City, she was in advertising, public relations and marketing at the time she ran the Iditarod. She later became marketing director for Outward Bound. Since her marriage to Ron Ellingson she has had the opportunity to pursue her interests and hobbies without the pressures and constraints of a job. In late 1985 she was on an extended tour with her dogs.

Her hobbies reflect her love for the outdoors. She loves to hike, camp, canoe and do other outdoor-related activities. She reads extensively. Her adventuresome spirit led her to participate in the ultimate. She did not finish but she tried, and in the best Alaskan tradition tested her frailties against the harshness of an Alaska winter along the Iditarod Trail.

Susan Butcher and Kathy Jones at race start. Jim Brown photo.

Below: Resting on the trail. Jim Brown photo.

Right: Rainy Pass, 1983 Iditarod Race. Photo courtesy of Connie Frerichs.

CHAPTER 4

New Women Entrants: 1978-1980

Nineteen hundred and seventy-eight marked a turning point in women's participation in the Iditarod Sled Dog Race. For the first time women placed in the top 20 finishers, placing in the money. One or more women have placed in the money every year since 1978.

In 1978 Varona Thompson became the first woman to race for the second time. Susan Butcher entered her first Iditarod in 1978, and has raced every year since compiling one of the best records for any racer in the race. Butcher and Thompson finished 19th and 20th in 1978.

Susan Butcher placed 9th in 1979, becoming the first woman to place in the top 10. 1980 saw the entrance of Libby Riddles who has done very well, always placing in the money. She became the first woman to win the Iditarod with her victory in 1985.

The 1978-1980 era marks the time when a number of women racers entered the Iditarod who have continued to race a number of years. Besides Butcher and Riddles these include Donna Gentry and Dee Dee Jonrowe. Susan Butcher continued her upward progress, finishing in 5th position in 1980. Donna Gentry placed 10th in 1980, her rookie year. Women racers were now beginning to be seen as serious contenders in the race.

SUSAN BUTCHER

Susan Butcher of Eureka, Alaska, has built a reputation as one of Alaska's foremost dog mushers. She has entered eight Iditarod races, and has placed in the money every time she has finished. She was the first woman to come in second, both in 1982 and 1984. She was the first woman to place in the money (19th in 1978); the first woman to place in the top 10 (9th in 1979); and the first woman to place in the top five (5th in 1980 and 1981). She has placed in the top 10 every year since 1979 except for 1985 when a moose attacked her team, killing two of her dogs and injuring 13 others. She scratched from the race.

Butcher and Joe Redington Sr., "Father of the Iditarod," together made another dog musher "first" when they took a dog team to the summit of Mt. McKinley on Memorial Day 1979. They learned dogs traveled consistently faster than people did. The dogs spent 45 minutes climbing a distance it took other climbers four hours to do.

Susan Butcher was born into a comfortable family life in Cambridge, Massachusetts. She spent childhood summers on the Maine sea coast, with "every waking hour learning and loving the outdoors."[1] Her favorite pet was her dog. As she grew older she yearned for a life that would put together her love of the outdoors and

Susan Butcher leaves 1983 Anchorage starting chute. R. Nielsen photo.

her love for dogs. She acquired her first Siberian huskies in Massachusetts. She made them pull, but had no sled for them.

She moved to Colorado in 1972. There she found the perfect match for her love of dogs and the outdoors — sled dog racing. She acquired a sled from a woman who had 50 dogs. "Within three minutes I moved in with her." Butcher handled dogs and competed in races there for three years. She yearned for a place where

> "I could breathe more freely and where my own hard work would be the measure of my success and the source of my existence."[1]

A veterinary technician, she came to Alaska to work at the University of Alaska musk oxen farm in 1975. She spent her first two Alaska winters living in the wilderness at Ptarmigan Lake in the Wrangell mountains building and and training a team for the 1978 Iditarod. She was 50 miles away from any road and 30 miles from her nearest neighbor. Her dogs included Tekla, who led her to the summit of Mt. McKinley and to Nome several times; Ivak; and Bubbs; along with one of her dogs from Colorado. "All I did was mush dogs."

Tekla, Butcher's lead dog, led her team in single lead "every inch of the way" for three Iditarods before being sidelined in the 1982 race due to bursitis.

> "Tekla is the one who taught me to mush. There isn't any one person who taught me even 1/50th of what Tekla taught me, and what Ivak (Tekla's brother) taught me."

Tekla was a year-old dog when Susan Butcher was freighting supplies in the Wrangells her first spring. She hauled about three tons 30 miles one way from a hunting cabin site to a lake, making two round trips a day. One warm spring day they were traveling along Beaver Creek on their way home. Tekla was in lead. Tekla suddenly went off the trail to the right. Susan told her to "Haw," but Tekla went right again. Susan again told her to haw, and Tekla, wanting to please, turned further to the left. They went another 20 feet when "a 50-foot section of ice dropped off below me and into a gushing, roaring river underneath. Luckily Tekla had gone far enough to the right to pull me out."

Butcher credits Tekla with saving her life a number of times. Such situations are how she learned total trust in her dogs, and a respect for their knowledge of a lot of things "I didn't have any idea about."

> "A lot of what Tekla and Ivak taught me was how to get across to a dog what I wanted."

A lot of times it almost seemed Tekla knew what Butcher wanted and would say, "No, I'm not going to do it if you ask me that way." Tekla and Ivak were Butcher's mainstays. Ivak was a wheel dog, pulling the sled, while Tekla led the team.

> "The worse the weather got, the more they liked it. The deeper the overflow, the more difficult the conditions, those two would be barking and just loved it."

Butcher has tried to instill that love of adverse conditions in her other dogs.

Tekla so loved and enjoyed running she didn't want to stop. Butcher would try to pull off the trail to take a nap. Tekla would express displeasure. Susan Butcher reports that all the years she had Tekla in lead she "never had any trouble." Tekla quit racing due to bursitis in her shoulder. Ivak continued and has gone to Nome seven times with Butcher. Tekla now helps train her puppies, and Ivak helps with her yearlings.

One of Butcher's greatest gifts is her "birth given ability" to work with animals. She feels she understands how they think which helps in her training of them. When she was in the Wrangells she was isolated from regular contacts with other people. There she put together a 15-dog team, and 11 of those dogs went with her on her first Iditarod. (She also leased two dogs from Patty Friend and two from Joe Redington Sr. for that Iditarod.)

While working with the University musk oxen herd at Unalakleet she met Joe Redington Sr. They talked about the Iditarod, and she told him about her dreams of running the Iditarod race. He invited her to come to Knik to train.

In late 1977 she went for what she planned as a two-week visit with Redington at Knik. She brought all her 15 dogs in her VW bug, and only had enough money for one week's dog food. She ended up staying the training season, and worked with Redington helping him train some puppies in exchange for some dog food.

The training camp was in the Knik-Goose Bay area where Shelley Gill and later Varona Thompson also trained for part of the time. Gill stayed in Butcher's tent at the training camp, and paid Susan with people food for training help. Butcher was fortunate to obtain a $3,000 sponsor to augment her meager resources. She devoted herself seriously and rigorously to her goal of becoming the best long distance musher, and was an apt pupil as her race record confirms.

Early in the 1978 race at Nine Mile Hill Susan came upon Varona Thompson, who had become entangled with a tree. Varona motioned Susan and other mushers on who offered her help as she didn't want to cause them any delay. Butcher still ended up banging her hand between a tree and her sled, and she continued on in the race in spite of the pain, even though she could only partially use her hand. Later her hand became infected.

Her toughness and determination helped her continue. She left Galena enroute to Nulato in a snowstorm. She and Charlie Fitka took turns breaking trail and made it to Nulato.

When Susan arrived at the finish line she beamed with happiness. Her father was there to greet her. She still had 6 of her original 14 dogs, 5 of whom were dogs she had trained in the Wrangell mountains. Her 19th place finish netted her $600, and began a record of women placing in the money every year since. She also was the 1978 Iditarod Trail Queen, and appeared at Nome and Anchorage banquets in a dress made from wool from musk oxen.

Since 1978 Butcher has believed in sled dog racing as a professional sport. Her goal is "to be the best in whatever I am doing." A tireless worker and professional long distance musher, she puts in 14 hour days, rarely taking a day off. In 1978 it was her dream to one day "be able to support myself and my dogs by dog mushing." Since 1981 she and her dog kennel have been self-sustaining, through dog sales, prize money, and occasional dog mushing related activities such as one-day trips hauling freight by dog team.

For quite a few years she feels she improved through watching top mushers and other mushers. She put together some of their racing technique, along with her knowledge of how to train dogs. It worked well for her. For the last six years she has been on her own. She tries new things. She feels her team has improved every year. Her breeding program has been very successful.

"It's endless energy, and endless time, and endless patience to get where those at the top have gotten."

She believes in putting all her energies into her goals and what she believes in. Her day begins early. At 6:00 a.m. she goes a quarter-mile to a running creek, her closest source of running water. She feeds her dogs a meat broth with vitamins before starting on the trail. She raises and breeds all her own dogs, and Tekla and Ivak are a major part of that breeding program.

Her dogs are descended from old-time Indian and Eskimo dogs bred for stamina and good feet that don't cut easily. They average about 50 pounds, and are of slender build with long legs. Each has a distinct personality. All love to run. Almost every dog she runs in her team now, she has raised. She has a lot of pride in that.

"There's a very special feeling between me and my dogs. I think they'd do most anything for me, and I know I'd do most anything for them."

Butcher starts working with her dogs from the time they are born. By age 5 weeks she takes them on daily walks. They are in and out of her house, and have free rein of the place until they reach 3 months of age. A special time each day is dedicated to her puppies. They go with her on three- to seven-mile hikes. She continues the daily walks when they are penned up at age 3 months. At age 4 months they are put on a chain. Two weeks later she starts them in harness. Every dog in her kennel is worked with daily.

Butcher enjoys every hour she spends with her dogs, and works daily with her puppies and yearlings as well as her team dogs. Although she has handlers to help her, she drives yearlings daily and feels "it is a fun part of the day." She puts in about eight hours behind a sled every day during the snow season, including time driving puppies which she "wouldn't give up for the world," even though it means an extra two hours of work a day.

In March 1979 Butcher raced in her second Iditarod. She placed 9th, again the highest finish for a woman, and earned $1,600. Not one to slack off, in April she and 10th place finisher Joe Redington Sr. started their dog team ascent of Mt. McKinley.

The two hauled much more gear than they needed on McKinley. Only she and Redington and four of the dogs actually went all the way together to the summit. Guide Ray Genet "showed us where to start, and we went on our own until 16,000 feet." Then they were joined by Genet.

Eight days before the actual climb to the top, their seven dogs had so much power Butcher put chains on the sled to slow them down. At one point she fell, and it was too steep for her to stop her team. Luckily they happened to run into Genet who "stopped us ten feet before a huge crevasse." Butcher was bruised, and the sled was broken. They decided to leave three dogs behind with a woman from another expedition who had altitude sickness. On one ascent it took about four hours to go about 700 yards. They had to pick out steps with an ice axe.

Their total time on Mt. McKinley was 44 days, including the days weathered in. It took only three days for the descent.

Butcher's life has been completely wrapped up in the Iditarod and long distance mushing since 1977. She carefully reviews each race's mistakes. In August preparations begin in earnest. Harnesses and sleds come out of storage and are carefully checked and prepared for use. Her dogs pull a wheeled cart over the bare ground in short training runs before the snows come to build up wind and endurance.

Butcher described her 1982 race preparations in a March 1983 *National Geographic* article. It listed her pre-Iditarod race tasks of packaging dog food in individual sacks for Iditarod Race Committee air drops to checkpoints along the trail. Their meat is cut in small chunks for easy feeding, and honey balls are made. Extra headlamp batteries, her own food, and gear are also stashed at checkpoints. Over a thousand handmade dog booties are sewn by Susan and friends. New harnesses, ganglines, plastic sled runners, lashings, and other supplies are gathered and custom fitted, along with hand sewn parkas, snow pants, and sturdy boots.[2]

She placed second in the 1982 Iditarod. However, early in the race she faced despair as a slide down an icy hill in the first miles caused injury to several dogs. Eight hours from the start, along the Yenta River, fresh snow obscured the trail. Cracker, Ruff, and Screamer began to limp. She loaded them into her sled. Continuing on she sensed something was wrong as she should have reached Skwentna.[3]

Soon a musher approached from the opposite direction with the news, "We're at least ten miles off course."[3] Turning around, she felt her hopes dashed. Tekla then began to limp. Four hours behind schedule she pulled into Skwentna. Dropping Cracker, Ruff and Screamer, she pushed on. Forty-five miles later she knew Tekla had reached her limit. With tears streaming down her cheeks, she dropped Tekla at Finger Lake.[3]

With only 11 dogs left she resolved to push on. Going through the 40-mile "burn" stretch of fire charred and fallen trees, heavy snows obscured the trail. She continued, catching up with the leaders who had lost their way and were waiting for daylight. Together the mushers took turns breaking trail in the deep, soft snow until conditions permitted them to travel on their own. For four-and-a-half days and 353 miles this tedious process continued.[4]

At Ruby, on the Yukon River, the weather temporarily improved. Butcher switched to a lighter sled. Temperatures dropped to −45 degrees. Frostbite was a real threat. While enroute along the 90-mile stretch to Unalakleet a raging storm moved in, hiding the trail. After taking overnight refuge in a trapper's tent, another day's mushing brought them to Unalakleet.[4]

Leaving Unalakleet for Shaktoolik her slow progress was hampered by high winds, dropping the visibility to zero. Her eyelashes and the dogs' eyelashes froze shut. She stopped often to clear their eyes and check their feet. Butcher was unable to see the tripod trail markers.[5]

Emmitt Peters and Herbie Nayokupuk joined her. Spacing their teams two feet apart they could not see to follow each other, and became separated. Butcher finally reached Shaktoolik, alone, with a frostbitten face. She waited there 52 hours. The storm abated slightly. Pushing through the continuing storm, seven lead teams traveled close together.[5]

Forty miles from Nome strong winds again assaulted the racers. Butcher's best lead dog, Ali, tired of taking commands. She switched Copilot to lead with Stripe. Her team increased its pace, driving hard. She was in 5th place.

She passed Ernie Baumgartner and Emmitt Peters. Stripe began to tire. She spent 40 seconds switching Ali back into lead. Repassing Peters, eight miles later she passed Jerry Austin. Rick Swenson was barely visible in the distance. She tried gamely but Swenson won by 3 minutes and 46 seconds, after 16 days on the trail. The crowd cheered her. She was $16,000 richer for her second place finish.[6]

Another Iditarod experience in 1984 showed how dangerous the race can be. Heading toward Shaktoolik there were no markers. Granite, her lead dog, was exhausted from geeing and hawing, looking for a trail or for the best terrain to travel on. They were on a lagoon. All of a sudden,

"The ice I was traveling on started billowing, and I realized I was on stuff that was only about a half-inch thick, but I had gotten out into the middle of a great big patch of it. . . . around me for hundreds of feet, the ice was just moving like waves. And I knew that shortly we were going to go through.

"I tried to stay calm. And then I quietly said to Granite, "Haw!" because that looked like it was the closest way to shore . . . all the dogs were getting real spooked. And he headed haw. And he just reached the shore at the time I went through. And as I went through the dogs started going through. But he was on the shore, and he was able to claw his way up and each additional group of dogs was able to get up and get them and us out of the water. Of course we got soaked."

Susan Butcher finished every Iditarod race she started until a cruel tragedy in 1985 forced her to scratch. The first night of the race, while cresting a hill, her team came upon a pregnant moose who viciously attacked her team, killing two of her dogs.

Butcher was mushing alone, in the lead. She sped along the windy, wooded trail to Rabbit Lake checkpoint. She rounded a corner and headed up a hill. Her dogs' ears went up. Her headlight beam then caught the moose.[7]

"Eyes wild, a large cow moose stood in the middle of the trail 20 feet in front of Granite. My heart pounding, I threw the sled over to a stop. The moose charged into the team, kicking and snorting . . . .[7]

"She stopped in the middle of the team and reared up on her hind legs, and with her full weight came crashing down on Johnnie and Ruff. . . . For the next five minutes, it was a nightmarish blur. I was hearing yelps of my beloved dogs, hearing the cow snorting and growling and the snaps of her hind legs striking out against dog after dog all up and down the line . . . .[7]

"Then suddenly she stopped, square in front of me. A reprieve for my dogs.

"I pulled off my parka, waving it in her face, trying to scare her off. She charged me. I backed off. But again I tried. She backed off to the front of the team where she had a free avenue of escape, but instead she charged again, pounding her front legs, this time on Hyde and Yeller.[8]

"Their screams tore through my heart. I ran forward with my axe, poking her with it, but she struck at me with her hind legs. I retreated and she calmed down for a few minutes.[9]

". . . I went slowly up through the team releasing necklines and tugs so the dogs tangled could retreat.[9]

"Then it started again. The moose charged, kicking wildly. Granite went for her hind legs. She got him in the head and he was thrown against a tree. She went after Copilot . . ."[9]

Then Butcher saw another light. Dewey Halverson came. He used his gun to shoot the moose who continued kicking until his last bullet finally killed her. Johnnie was dead. "Hyde was gasping for air, his gums white."[9] The other dogs were standing. Seven had head wounds. Butcher wrapped Hyde in her sleeping bag.

Butcher, Halverson, and Glen Findlay gutted the moose as required by Iditarod and state laws. She asked Halverson to go ahead and send a snowmachine back for her. He insist-

Susan Butcher. Jim Brown photo.

ed she go on ahead so the four other teams could follow her in case she needed help. At her command her team enthusiastically moved ahead, although more slowly than before. She arrived at Rabbit Lake and, after agonizing over what happened, she scratched from the race, as 15 of her 17 dogs were injured.[9]

Hyde was flown to Anchorage for emergency surgery. Despite five hours of surgery he died from injuries to his liver. His brothers, Luke and Yeller, also had surgery.[9] Both have recovered, and Susan is training them for her 1986 Iditarod team. In spite of her pain and agony, while in Anchorage for veterinary care for her injured dogs, she spent many hours at Iditarod race headquarters. There she helped out, answering phones and providing background information about the trail to volunteers working during the race.

Butcher entered the Coldfoot Classic in April 1985, only weeks after the above moose encounter. A testimony to her prowess with her dogs is that she won that race. She was only able to use 8 of the 17 dogs she had started in the 1985 Iditarod in the Coldfoot race. Butcher raced several dogs she had retired from the Iditarod, some young dogs, and two pregnant dogs she had not taken on the Iditarod. All her dogs came through "with flying colors," and she had a lot of fun during the Coldfoot race.

For the 1986 racing season she will be racing the John Beargrease Race in Minnesota. She, Libby Riddles, and Rick Swenson (four-time Iditarod winner) have all been invited to the race, and are being paid by some supporters of the race to participate. In addition, she will run the Kusko 300 or another 200-mile race as well as the 1986 Iditarod and possibly the Coldfoot Classic.

Butcher feels Libby Riddles' victory in the 1985 Iditarod did not interfere with her goals as she did not have a chance to compete against Riddles in that race. She continues her pursuit of her goal of being the best long-distance musher, which has been systematically pursued to the exclusion of any hobbies.

In spite of maintaining a strict schedule of training during the fall and winter months, Butcher has continued to be involved in her concerns for the welfare of musk oxen. In early fall 1985 she was in the Anchorage area to add her input and support to a suit over care of these special animals.

On August 31, 1985, a special event took place at Butcher's kennel in Eureka. On a sunny afternoon Susan Butcher and David Monson exchanged wedding vows. The wedding mixed traditional and non-traditional aspects. The ring bearers were her lead dogs Tekla and Granite, under the watchful control of two of her sisters.[10]

Her bridesmaids included close friends Kathy Jones and Rick Swenson, her arch competitor in the Iditarod. Her husband's best man was a woman. Dressed in a traditional white satin dress, vows were exchanged outside among the beauty of nature and in a ceremony blending traditional words and original writings. After the ceremony the reception was a mixture of traditional and homespun Alaskan-style fun. When the festivities wound down at midnight a rain shower came.[10]

Susan Butcher represents the best of mushing in the Alaskan tradition. Her persistence and success have elevated her and the Iditarod race to new heights. Her dedication to her profession has led her to participate as an Iditarod Trail Committee board member for several years, where she speaks up forcefully and effectively. Her drive there has been to see the committee put in a decent race trail so no dogs or mushers have to risk their lives to any greater extent than is necessary.

She willingly promotes the race by appearing at the State Fairs and other fund raising and support activities. Most of all she is a warm, family oriented person whose hard work and dedication has made her a success in her chosen profession.

Butcher's determination is shown in her ability to turn potential disasters into accomplishments. Last year she was using a Honda four-wheel vehicle for training her dogs prior to the snows. One day she took a seldom used trail. In turning her team around to head home, her inexperienced leader went "gee" when Butcher commanded "Haw!", dragging Butcher, the four-wheeler, and the team down a 12-foot drop into 10-foot-tall alders. Butcher lacked a saw, axe, or other good tree cutting tool.

It was blowing and snowing lightly. The temperature was −20 degrees. She knew it would be one or two days before anyone would find her there. With only pliers, a wrench, and a screwdriver with a broken handle she spent four-and-a-half hours chopping down three-inch-diameter alders to make a path out of the area. She had her team pull the machine up the hill a foot at a time. Then she'd cut more trees, and had the dogs pull some more until they reached the top. After five hours they were safe, and enroute home. Her ability to turn difficult situations such as this into successful conclusions is one of the reasons she is a success.

SHELLEY GILL

Shelley Gill Vandiver ran the 1978 Iditarod race and finished 29th in a field of 40 drivers. A journalist who is currently the publisher of the *Frontiersman* and *Valley Sun* newspapers, Gill has covered five Iditarods as a member of the press. In 1984 Gill published a children's book entitled *Kiana's Iditarod*; a look at the race from the dog's point of view.

It was Antarctic explorer and adventurer Norman Vaughan who first encouraged Gill to run the Iditarod.

"I don't remember why I decided to do it, but it sounded like fun. I was always fascinated by (Jack) London. I'm a writer. I thought it would make a good tale to tell. I was just starting as a journalist then, but more than anything it sounded like a lot of fun."

Shelley Gill. Photo courtesy of S. Gill.

Vaughan was celebrating his 75th birthday the year Gill decided to try the race. He had been forced to scratch in two previous Iditarod attempts, but his name was on the sign-up sheet for the 1978 race. Gill wanted to see Vaughan make it to Nome. They camped together early in the race. As her team outdistanced his, she began to pack down the snow at her campsites and as she pulled out he would pull in. Vaughan's leg was in a cast from a training injury, and Gill felt sure he could make it to Nome if he could get through the deep snow areas encountered early in the race. Vaughan made it to Nome in 1978 in 33rd position. Since then he has gone on to complete two more Iditarods.

Gill was one of three women to race in 1978. Susan Butcher, Varona Thompson and Gill all trained together early in the training season at the Goose Bay Camp of Joe Redington Sr. Gill remembers Butcher as a fierce competitor, and Varona as "tenacious as a bull dog." At that time Gill's winter camping skills were not yet well developed. She recalls being just "one stick ahead of the fire." She recalls that she and some others

> "used to run out in the morning clad only in long johns to hack at spruce trees for their breakfast wood."

Looking back on her early training days she recalls Joe Sr. gave a great many pointers to the serious mushers at his camp. "He didn't take me very seriously, and at the time I guess I wasn't," says Gill. But as the snow conditions at the Knik area camp deteriorated, Gill decided to move her training ground north. She stayed at a friend's cabin on the Brushkana River where it crossed the Denali Highway. "That was where I learned to drive dogs," she says.

Her most "hair raising" Iditarod experience didn't occur in the race itself. It came in the middle of training when Gill needed more dogs, after a dog fight injured three members of her team during a preliminary race.

She and a friend set out in a jeep for Manley. No one mentioned the road was closed in the winter. When they discovered it was closed they decided to continue. The road was glaciated, and at one spot they didn't have enough speed as they climbed a steep hill. They began to slide backwards on the ice. Her friend decided to get out. Setting one foot outside she found she couldn't get any traction either. Back in she came. After steering like mad in reverse, Gill backed down the side of that mountain. Gathering more speed they went up it again. Eventually they made it to Rick Swenson's place in Eureka.

It was -60 degrees the next morning, and they had to build a fire under the jeep to get it going. Coming back was easier "as we had tracks to follow." In the end the dogs from Swenson did not pan out.

In 1978 food drops were made to the checkpoints two weeks before the race. Gill had prepared some delicious snacks for herself with smoked salmon. By the time she picked up her food at Susitna there had been considerable thawing and freezing. The smoked salmon spoiled, and Gill got a bad case of food poisoning.

She had experiences similar to most mushers. She was lost for 18 hours in Rainy Pass when she got off the trail in whiteout conditions. She met up with a couple of guys who didn't want a woman to finish ahead of them. After leading two of them across the ice from Unalakleet, the men sneaked out of Solomon, the last checkpoint. They had gone out "to water their dogs" but soon she saw their headlamps bobbing in the distance. She passed one right away because he didn't have any leader, and beat them both to the finish line even though she had to pass one on Nome's Front Street.

She started the race with 13 dogs. She crossed the finish line with seven dogs. She dropped two dogs in Unalakleet because they were tired. They "weren't happy anymore." She knew they could make it to Nome, but felt it would be better for the dogs if they were not pushed.

Her dogs came from several sources. She leased dogs from several mushers. Most of her dogs were a Joe Redington Jr. and Joe Redington Sr. (Tennessee) mix. She went through 56 dogs before she found the lucky 13. (She no longer has her own team. After the race she sold her dogs to Carla and Ray Lang. These dogs and their pups have won a number of races along the coast. She tries to visit the Langs annually and take the dogs out to keep her mushing skills intact.)

Gill, Patty Friend and Libby Riddles each had the same major sponsor from 1978 to 1981. Ed Clinton of Anchorage sponsored them. He was a loyal sponsor of women who wanted to compete in the Iditarod.

Little in her early childhood prepared her for the adventures of dog mushing and the Iditarod. Born in Albuquerque, New Mexico, she moved to south Florida at the age of 10. She was a "surfer" girl who spent her days on the beach though her family was not particularly outdoor oriented. But she describes the key to her later adventuresome spirit as the message her mother drilled into her as a child: "I could do anything I wanted to."

At age 17 she left home. Making her way to New Orleans, she worked on the switchboard at a crisis clinic.

She also took tourist photographs for a night club on Bourbon Street. She was an anti-war protestor who had "wanted to come to Alaska since I was 17." In 1974 she and her husband were living in the South. They decided to take a year off for traveling and came to Alaska. She has never left. Her marriage dissolved after her Iditarod adventure.

Gill has some definite ideas about the race. It is a special test — a kind of celebration for most drivers. When you finish:

"What you feel is really kind of lucky that you lived because there were a lot of potentially dangerous situations. You think it would be real possible to get in serious trouble out there. It's kind of a leveler, but at the same time it builds character. It builds self-esteem.

"I decided real soon I would never be a contender in this race because I wasn't tough enough and I liked my dogs too much. I just enjoyed them a lot. I had one sleep in the sleeping bag with me nearly every night. You have to push. You really have to drive to win.

"In my opinion there are two kinds of mushers. There are the ones who drive harder than hell to win at the expense of everything. And there are drivers who do so much preparation and are so good at what they do, and their dogs are so happy and good that they come out on top. And that's why I am so glad that Libby won because she's that kind of driver. She loves her dogs. You know she's a good driver. She takes good care of her dogs. Joe Garnie is the same way."

Gill finds March a tough month. She would like to run the race again. However, the commitment needed to do it is not something she is willing to make right now.

"Running the Iditarod is probably the easiest thing I ever did in my life. It was the most fun . . . .

It's hard not to (do) because it was a lot of fun. It was immediate gratification. People think it was very hard. But what could be easier than not having to worry about all that day-to-day garbage that we worry about? Not having a house. Not having to worry about that stuff. All you had to worry about was getting on a sled and going forward. And it was great. And you got all these pats on the back for doing something that was really an adventure and fun and really neat. So, sure I'd like to run it again for that reason. I'd love to run it again to photograph it. I'd love to run it again to do better — not faster. To have it easier cause I've learned a lot more."

Shelley Gill likes adventures. She views herself as a motivating type person. She has achieved the top of her field as far as small newspapers are concerned. Gill likes photo journalism, and is considering future options. One firm plan is to cover the 1986 Iditarod as a member of the press. Noting "nothing is more relaxing than driving a dog team," she drove Norman Vaughan's 1985 team back the 60 miles to Knik after an injury forced him to scratch from the race at Rabbit Lake.

PATTY FRIEND

When Patty Friend took to the trail in the 1979 Iditarod race much was expected of her. Her husband, Rod Perry, had run the race three times and each time placed in the money (17th in 1973, 14th in 1974, and 19th in 1977). Patty had just won the 1979 Cantwell 200 beating out prerace favorite 1976 Iditarod champion Jerry Riley of Nenana.

Friend's interest in running the Iditarod race grew from watching the race and from helping her husband train his 1977 race team. Her love of dogs and dog sled travel has much earlier roots. As an instructor in winter courses for the National Outdoor Leadership School in Wyoming, her students carried 70-pound packs while skiing. That weight was tough for those just getting acquainted with skis. So she and other staff began using a dog team to lighten individual loads.

Leaving the Knik checkpoint late the evening of the first day of the 1979 Iditarod race, Patty traveled into the wee hours of the morning without a working headlight. After hours on the trail without seeing another musher she began to think she had taken a wrong fork at some point. Near dawn, much to her relief, she came upon two camped mushers outside of Susitna Station.

The next morning she was feeding her dogs. One dog chewed a line. She began mending the line. Her team was grouped around her. A passerby remarked that they looked like "a little prayer group."

As she neared the finish line she began to feel sad. The race and goal of the past two years were almost over. Also, after more than 17 days on the trail, sharing a variety of experiences with her dogs, an incredible bond develops between the dogs and driver. Arriving in Nome, in the money, in 20th position, she was separated from her dogs. No longer was her bed a sled near her faithful companions!

She feels there is a satisfaction in meeting the challenge of the race. She overcame being lost on the Yukon River enroute to Greyling when a search party was sent to find her when she was long overdue. She survived various weather conditions and physical discomforts. She also states she will probably never run it again. She feels it takes so much in the way of resources — physical, emotional, financial, etc. — to field a competitive team. There are other things she would prefer to do now.

The four dogs on Friend's Chugiak dog lot today are a far cry from the larger team that logged 2,500 miles in training. The rigid four-hours-running and four-hours-resting schedule she set for the Iditarod race is light-years away from her relaxed attitude of recreational dog mushing followed these days. In retrospect, she feels she trained too hard and that she and the dogs entered the race fatigued. She feels she, and possibly others, placed too much emphasis on finishing position. Looking back now, Patty states she would put fewer miles on the dogs in training and approach the race with a lighter attitude.

Patty's own nature allows her to appreciate the countryside and the history of the trails she travels. Following the race, she worked for a

Patty Friend at 1983 All-Alaska Sweepstakes drawing. Jim Brown photo.

number of months mapping the Iditarod National Trail for the Bureau of Land Management's (BLM's) National Historic Trails Project. For this she talked with old timers and people along the trail, and worked with long forgotten maps to pinpoint the original trails. Excited when viewing historic photographs, she enjoys feeling part of Alaska's unique history and heritage.

In 1983 Friend was the only female musher among 23 participants in a race commemorating the 75th anniversary of the Nome to Candle "All Alaska Sweepstakes." A 408-mile race, it followed the rules and trail of the famous race that took place in Nome between 1908 and 1917. Her face lights up as she describes that adventure. "The land was breathtaking in only that special way the Northland is." She felt history as she mushed. Describing climbing up and down the rugged hills into valley after valley, she called it a "tough course."

The All Alaska Sweepstakes was especially tough on Patty physically because she had strep throat before and during the race. On the trail, 70 miles into the race, the infection recurred. It also infected her eyes. Although it was a struggle to complete the race, she placed 17th. Her entry fee of $1,000 in gold dust was repaid many times over in the experiences she had and the memories. Of equal satisfaction, though, was enjoying the race even under the circumstances, not taking the entire situation so seriously, and having "a bit more fun."

Patty attributes her love of dogs and of the outdoors to her upbringing. The oldest of four girls, she grew up in Colorado Springs, Colorado. Her parents owned a furniture and appliance store there. She learned to hunt with her father. The family was outdoors oriented, and there were many family camping trips and outdoors activities. There were always at least one or two pet dogs. She also had a horse. When she raced in the 1979 Iditarod, her parents, now retired in Oregon, came up around Thanksgiving and stayed through March, helping with the many race preparations.

Friend came to Alaska in 1971. She and a friend drove the highway with three sled dogs, a sled, and a canoe. She taught 30-day kayaking courses on Prince William Sound. She had a recreational sled dog team near Cantwell, on the border of the then-McKinley Park. During summers she worked first for the National Outdoor Leadership School and later for the National Park Service.

In 1974 she moved to Anchorage to pursue a master's degree in counseling psychology. (She has a BA in psychology from Colorado State University.) Employed in a work study job as a carpenter's helper by the Bureau of Land Management (BLM), she enjoyed this "delightful job" immensely — so much that although she finished her academic coursework she never completed her thesis. Instead she remained with the BLM until 1983 as a carpenter.

Rod Perry and Patty were divorced in 1981. Today John Cruickshank and Patty share a home in Birchwood. They have a small business doing electrical, heating, plumbing, and carpentry work. Their lifestyle is a blending of the old and new. The rural residential neighborhood consists of large lots and an atmosphere in which there is room for horses, and dog lots abound. Nearby there is undeveloped park land and the Chugiak sled dog trails. Birchwood is only 30 minutes away from downtown Anchorage.

In 1983-84 John and Patty built a cabin and spent the winter a few miles out of Talkeetna. Patty is currently studying and assisting teaching stress management and yoga in addition to her business.

Patty Friend points out that, always, dog mushing means dogs. Some of those dogs she has trained and raced, and those she now owns, have come out of the great Alaskan tradition of tough, fast dogs bred for the sled. Behind her dogs are the generations of dog breeding by villagers and, later, by such mainstays of the dog driving tradition as Joe Redington Sr. and Jerry Riley. Dogs out of this pool of exceptional talent are running with great distinction on the teams of race leaders like Libby Riddles. Patty is proud of her dogs and their breeding and her part in continuing their line. She feels that one of the great privileges of serious dog mushing has been living and working with these fine animals.

DONNA GENTRY

Donna Gentry, 1980 Iditarod rookie of the year, placed 10th of the 62 mushers who entered that year. She again placed in the money in 1981 in 18th position. Donna, a vibrant, dedicated person, began sled dog racing as a youngster in Laconia, New Hampshire. In 1976 Gentry finished second in the Anchorage Open World Championship Race, the highest finish ever for a woman.

Originally a sprint racer, she started long distance mushing after moving to Skwentna, Alaska, in 1977. She lived 12 miles from her closest neighbor. That first year was hard to change her team from a sprint orientation to a long distance one. The dogs "were convinced that at the end of the road, at the end of the trail, there was going to be the dog truck or their dog houses."

As a youngster she lived in Laconia, New Hampshire, the home of the Laconia World Sled Dog Racing championships. The races started on Main Street and went through town passing her house. Watching the race she saw Jean Bryar, well known sprint racer, go by. Gentry thought, "if she can do it with her team I can do it with my poodle." So she did. She trained for a whole year. That winter her father bought her a used sled. In February she entered her first dog race. She won the second place trophy in the one dog class against "all those huskies" with her standard poodle.

After hooking up her family's pet beagle and cocker spaniel with her poodle, her father decided it was time to get her some huskies. Her first three huskies came from Jean Bryar. She ran the three-dog class and then the five-dog class. At age 13 she became a last minute entrant in the Laconia World Championship Race when a friend who had entered hurt his knee. He asked her to run his team in the race. Using her own lead dog plus her swing dogs and his team, she placed 13th in a race with over 30 entrants. Looking back she states, "I had a fantastic leader." Nugget accompanied her to Alaska when she moved here in 1968, the day after she finished high school.

To Donna the beauty of a dog team is "poetry in motion." You see every pair of dogs right together and the same foot of every dog is hitting the ground at the same time. At first it was difficult for her to see the beauty of the long distance trotting pace as in sprint races dogs run for speed. Trotting, a slower pace, is "horror" to a sprint racer.

Donna's commitment to the Iditarod is a year-round one. Since 1980 she has served on the Iditarod Trail Committee Board. In 1984 she served as a race judge. In 1985 she served as race marshall, the first year the race was temporarily stopped for any reason. It was a very difficult decision to make. Freezing the race at Rainy Pass due to the lack of dog food at Rohn River and Nikolai went against the philosophy of the Iditarod race. "It went against everything the Iditarod stood for." It was a direct intervention in the race. It took away all the musher's choices. In the end she made the decision in terms of safety — safety for both mushers and their dogs due to the lack of food. It was not halted for lack of trail.

She feels the second freeze was more controversial. At Rainy Pass the leaders had been there long enough to leave if they had so desired. All the mushers had arrived there. At the time of the second race halt there were a couple of teams heading to Ophir, with no communications to Ophir, before she became aware there was no dog food at Iditarod. There was no way to get food to Ophir. In spite of all the problems she is willing to serve as a race official again "because of the mushers."

Reflecting on the two Iditarods she has run, Donna notes that her Iditarod lead dog Pup Pup was not her original leader. That dog, Rosy, died suddenly the summer of 1979. When she previously had tried to train Pup Pup as a leader along with Rosy, Pup Pup was not very responsive. After Rosy's death when the first snow came, Pup Pup took over. "She decided to play leader." Donna didn't have a lot of confidence in her because of her earlier non-cooperation.

In 1980 in the Burn area there was no snow. Near Egypt Mountain they were climbing and climbing. There

Donna Gentry and lead dog Pup-Pup. R. Nielsen photo.

was nothing for a trail. It was just grass with frozen water, "high mountain tundra swamp." Donna was totally convinced they were lost. It started getting real icy. Pup Pup wanted to go straight across a glacier. Gentry couldn't see any flag or glaze or evidence of a trail that way. She and Pup Pup had a "first class argument." Finally the dog gave in. She went where Donna wanted to go. It was a dead end. They had to turn the sled on end and back out. They then proceeded up the bank Pup Pup had chosen earlier. At the top of the bank there was a marker. Pup Pup went up to it. She looked back at Donna and smiled just like "I told you so." "It was funny," recalls Donna.

Pup Pup again showed her ability to find the invisible trail when they came over Topkok Hill. Pup Pup kept wanting to go to the left — towards the sea ice. Donna kept saying, "Gee!" Her lead dog kept fighting her. Then they came on the road. Gentry thought you didn't hit the road till Safety and assumed they had missed Safety. She turned the team around and headed back. Things didn't seem right. Pup Pup was really fighting her. Pup Pup was right. (The road was five miles before Safety.) She let two teams get ahead of her because "I was too stubborn to listen to my dog."

Gentry attributes her 10th place success to Pup Pup. She feels she was too conservative as she was afraid she'd burn her team out; so conservative that "I had a dog team that loped up Front Street."

Reflecting on her experiences, Gentry notes, "it's not very often dogs let you down." It's not often they make mistakes. "It's the mushers who make the bad decisions." She feels the Iditarod really showed her what her dogs can do. Her 1980 team was the same team she used in sprint races. Yet Iditarod showed her much more of the dog's personalities and abilities. She feels the Iditarod has so much. "When you first get to Nome it's great, but you appreciate the race more five months after you finished it than you do during it."

In 1980 she came over Topkok Hill at sunset. The whole Bering coast was pink. Everything was outlined in mounds of pink with purple shades. "It made the whole race worth it, just something like that. Even now I think about that." There were other special things. A certain night with the dogs, the way a dog did something special for you. By 1981 Pup Pup was selecting their campsites. She'd find a good place she could get into and out of without a hassle and off she'd go. In 1981 Pup Pup took Libby Riddles and Jerry Riley and Gentry across the Burn. Riddles nominated Pup Pup for lead dog of the year.

For Gentry one of the neatest things about dog mushing is that "it's an equal sport." Most of the things connected with it don't matter if you are male or female. She feels that dog mushing for her personally kept her out of trouble as a kid. Also, working with animals (and not just dogs) gives one a lot of "respect for other people." You have to understand the animals to perform well. You have to understand yourself. She feels the adults in Laconia were real encouraging. They helped you out even when you did better than they did in races. They still were always happy for you. She belonged to the New England Sled Dog Racing Association. She was the first woman to win that club's trophy for highest number of points (1966).

She feels it is hard for a mother to run the Iditarod. "You have to play super mom." Living in remote locations makes it harder.

In October 1985 the Gentrys moved to Palmer, Alaska. Her goals now center around her children. Thirteen-year-old Robin (who ran the Junior Rondy in 1982) is now into horses. Two-year-old Crispin keeps her active. Although she no longer has her dog team, she still has Pup Pup plus a black lab puppy. She misses her familiar Skwentna surroundings. Being near a larger community she hopes to be more active in community activities such as PTA, 4-H, and other family related activities. She feels her proximity to Iditarod headquarters will allow more active committee involvement. Her husband, Lloyd, continues to work on the North Slope. His new job duties prompted their relocation to the Matanuska Valley.

Donna Gentry has given much to the Iditarod. It has given much to her. Her positive attitude and willingness to involve herself as musher and as Iditarod official have been invaluable. Her early success in sprint racing and her Iditarod achievements mark her as a remarkable person in dog driving circles.

LIBBY RIDDLES

"LIBBY WINS!" That triumphant line was repeated over and over when 28-year-old Libby Riddles of Teller, Alaska, arrived victoriously in Nome on March 20, 1985, to claim the $50,000 first prize in the Iditarod Race. This independent, adventuresome, attractive lady shocked top male mushers by leaving Shaktoolik in a howling windstorm a few days earlier. Her daring gamble paid off, thrusting her into the limelight.

Riddles moved to Alaska in 1973, shortly before her 17th birthday. During her early years in Alaska she lived in the rural fringes around Anchorage. She worked as a night watchman for the BLM (Bureau of Land Management) and at other seasonal jobs.

In 1975 she began running dogs. She and Duane "Dewey" Halverson purchased dogs from musher friends Rod Perry and Patty Friend and exchanged much information with them. She credits Friend and Rod and Alan Perry as being a big influence on her. An avid reader, she read everything she could find on caring for and racing sled dogs. She also learned much from watching other mushers. However, she feels she learned more from the dogs she raced in her first Iditarod race in 1980 than she learned from any one person.

In 1977 Halverson raced in the Iditarod race. Libby's interest in the Iditarod was sparked by his participation in the race. When the two parted company shortly after the race, Riddles retained seven or eight dogs. Later she moved alone to a cabin at Nelchina where she gained comfort in dealing with Alaskan winters. Those winters alone at Nelchina strengthened her independence and will.

Riddles first ran the Iditarod in 1980. She left the starting line with 14 dogs. A very organized, meticulous person when it comes to her dogs, she began the previous summer planning logistics for her race. She sewed booties, harnesses, and did her race "homework." She kept careful records on her dogs in training, recording the mileage she logged on them. She ran them thousands of miles preparing for the race.

Support from family and friends (mostly from Nelchina and the BLM) embraced her as she prepared for her first Iditarod. Her mother traveled from Phoenix to Anchorage to follow her progress along the trail, and flew to Nome to greet her at the finish line. Her sister made her dress for the Anchorage mushers' banquet. Alaskan brother Michael made a cooker for her dog food. BLM friends provided some of her personal race food. When Libby reached Nome at 10:45 p.m. on St. Patrick's Day she had 11 of her 14 dogs in harness after 16 days on the trail. (Five dogs were 10 years old!) Her efforts were rewarded with $650 for placing 18th.

She remembers traveling from Kaltag to Unalakleet with Harold Ahmasuk. Enroute he built a big bonfire. Later she arrived in White Mountain in 21st position at midnight. Five mushers were sleeping. She stayed only the mandatory one-hour layover time. An hour after she left she was passed by Rudy Demoski and Dave Olson, but she never was passed by the other three mushers she left at White Mountain. While

Libby Riddles. Jim Brown photo.

snacking her dogs she was met by Harold Ahmasuk. They battled for the lead into Safety. She won. He then allowed her to arrive first in Nome.

Riddles raced again in 1981. She had a better race than the previous year but only placed 20th. Her financial reward was slightly better at $1,000. The early part of the race was tough as around Rohn River and the Farewell Burn there was not much snow. She traveled in part with 1980 Rookie of the Year Donna Gentry until Unalakleet when Donna started "pouring the coals to it" leaving Libby behind. Reflecting on her 1981 race she feels her dogs did better and she had a more efficient run than in 1980. Both parents of her current lead dog raced that year for her. Only one dog, Big Bane, from her 1981 team is still racing. In 1980 and 1981 three women — Susan Butcher, Donna Gentry and Libby — all finished in the money.

In 1981 Libby spent the summer working at Shaktoolik. That same year she moved to Teller, Alaska, a windswept coastal village of about 250 persons northwest of Nome, at the invitation of Joe Garnie. Libby feels the relocation to Teller was important. She feels Teller has good weather for training dogs because the weather is bad, and it makes them tough. There she and Garnie raise all their own dogs. "It is a pretty good feeling to have raised dogs yourself that can win. It is fun to watch them grow up." She took 13 to 15 dogs to Teller plus "lots of pups." Her current leader and brothers were born shortly after her move to Teller. Joe and Libby train dogs together. The team that led her to victory was virtually the same team raced by Joe Garnie when he placed third in the Iditarod race in 1984. Half of those 16 dogs belong to Libby.

Libby started the 1985 race in 46th position with 15 dogs. Eighteen days later she arrived with 13 dogs in harness in first place in Nome. The first musher into Eagle Island, over 400 miles from Nome, she allowed several mushers to leave ahead of her. Second to reach the coast at Unalakleet (about 270 miles from Nome), she again took the lead. She never again relinquished it, stating:

"Keep racing out of checkpoints when the guys are checking in, that's the way to do it."[11]

She took off in the predawn darkness for Shaktoolik, 40 miles away, arriving there at 2:17 p.m. Just three hours later, shortly after Lavon Barve's arrival, she took off in a howling windstorm saying:

"It took a long time to get here going in the wind. That's how going across the bay will be, too."[12]

After departing into the vicious winds and storm, no word of her progress came until late next morning when a plane spotted her. After leaving Shaktoolik she drove her team 10 to 15 miles into the wind. She found she could not see well enough to follow the trail after it got dark. Stopping next to a trail marker, she threw everything out of her sled. She crawled into her sleeping bag inside her sled bag. It took her two hours to change out of her wet gear into dry clothes. Forty-mile-per-hour winds lashed at her sled.

About 10 a.m. the next morning a mail plane flew overhead. Its presence slightly angered her as she thought, "Now they will know how close to Shaktoolik I am."[13]

Forcing herself up, after gulping down a chocolate bar and seal oil, she headed for Koyuk. She stopped often to wipe snow from her dogs' eyes and give them snacks. At 5:15 p.m. on Monday, March 18th, a jubilant Riddles and dog team entered the fishing village of Koyuk, 58 miles from Shaktoolik. She commented, "It was cold and miserable."[14]

That afternoon her closest competitors departed Shaktoolik. Duane Halverson and John Cooper arrived on Norton Bay in the dark. The trail markers were difficult to locate. By chance when one turned off his headlamp the lights of Koyuk were visible. They arrived after midnight, a couple hours after Libby's departure. She had a five-hour lead on them. In White Mountain after completing her mandatory layover, no other mushers had arrived. She stated:

> "I still don't believe it. I'm going to have to cross the finish line first. We could have an earthquake or tidal wave you know."[15]

Enroute down the coast she lost her way. She spotted her own tracks on the trail in the darkness.

> "I followed a staked trail that led to Solomon, instead of Safety where the checkpoint is, putting on an extra 10 to 15 miles. I got turned around when I departed Solomon, but figured it out in just a few miles."

When Libby reached the last checkpoint at Safety she did an unheard of thing for a front-runner. Only 22 miles from Nome she lingered, where most mushers push hard to make the best time possible. It had been a tough night on the dogs, in the wind, and she wanted to take it easy on them. She knew the nearest teams were five hours behind her yet. The trail from White Mountain was "pretty tough" and her dogs needed a rest. Her two leaders were nestled in the back of a snowmobile making themselves comfortable. Libby laid down for about 20 minutes, resting and napping.

True to her word, people in Nome did not have to get up in the wee hours of the night to greet her. Shortly after 9 a.m. on Wednesday, March 20th, Libby Riddles drove down Front Street to the finish line. "What I feel like is if I die now, it's okay,"[16] she spontaneously quipped to the hundreds of cheering onlookers who greeted her. She saluted Axle and Dugan, her faithful lead dogs, promising all her dogs a steak and a box of dog biscuits. $50,000 richer, more than twice the money ever garnered by an Iditarod winner, she won the hearts of thousands. A winning portrait of Libby and her lead dogs now hangs in United States embassies around the world.

Libby, a modest, down to earth, lovely person, is quick to give credit to her dogs. The dogs are real heroes themselves. Without them there would be no race. She is understandably proud of her dogs — and even prouder yet that she and Joe Garnie have bred and raised them themselves.

Her four year hiatus from the Iditarod race was not a break from racing. It was a time of preparation. She ran the Kusko 300 in 1982 and 1984. Her meticulous attention to detail paid off. Her courageous gamble allowed the unexpected to happen. From a little known contender she was vaulted out of obscurity into the limelight by her victory.

Who would have guessed this youngster who came to Alaska just before her 17th birthday would 12 years later become one of its most famous citizens? The second of seven children of professor Willard and Mary Riddles, this heroine was not always viewed as an athlete.

As a youngster she spent a lot of time in the woods, although she did little hiking or sports activities. She always had pets. At age 7 or 8 she and her dog were inseparable. She attended a university campus school and a few other good elementary schools. She credits them with teaching her how to self-educate herself. To some extent the ability to learn things through books gave her the confidence to tackle other goals. This educational process has become the backbone of her way of approaching many important aspects in her life.

Since her victory Libby's life has changed. She has had to make choices about endorsements, speeches, and lending her support to many good causes. The pressures of stardom have not changed her basic outlook. She has become a role model for young children and an inspiration, neither of which she had foreseen as happening to her. While home in Teller, however, she still finds time to play with her cat, Danger, and to listen to music which she enjoys.

Libby Riddles leaves Anchorage at start of 1985 Iditarod Race. Jim Brown photo.

She also sews a lot. She makes a lot of things from fur, especially fur hats. Her fur hats are well known and desired by many. She donated one to the Iditarod Trail Committee, which was sought after by many individuals in a drawing for it.

Libby feels she can call herself "an Alaskan now."[17] She is pleased with the attention her victory has given the sport of dog mushing. She has been generous in promoting dog mushing and the Iditarod race. In January she will journey to Minnesota for the John Beargrease Race, a 400-mile event. Libby, Susan Butcher, and four-time Iditarod winner Rick Swenson are being paid by some race supporters to compete in the event. However, Libby will not be among those entered in the 1986 Iditarod. It is Joe Garnie's turn to race their team in the 1986 Iditarod.

On September 23, 1985, in ceremonies in New York City, Libby Riddles accepted the award as professional Sportswoman of the Year from the Women's Sports Foundation. She was a guest on "Good Morning America."

What does the future hold for her? She is hard at work on a book about her life, and has offers to make a movie. She is working and training a group of 2-year-old dogs along with the "veterans." She is also raising pups.

Most of all Libby remains a beautiful young woman who is an inspiration. She has advanced the cause of her sport, dog mushing. The headline "Libby Riddles Named the Best"[18] indeed sums up the affection and admiration of Alaskans for her.

DEE DEE JONROWE

Dee Dee Jonrowe of Bethel, Alaska, a vivacious, outgoing individual, has entered and finished four Iditarod races. Her 1983 15th-place finish has been her best performance to date. Working in Bristol Bay and Southeast Alaska as a buyer representative for Kemp Pacific Fisheries, she fishes her own gill net boat in her home area. She enjoys traveling by dog team to different areas of Alaska.

Dee Dee has always liked dogs. Her first one was given to her at age 6 weeks. The daughter of a career military family she traveled extensively as a youngster. She always had pets. Instead of dolls she had animals which she toted around. These included guinea pigs in Ethiopia for whom she even had clothing.

Her family moved to Alaska in 1971. She had to sell her horses. So she gravitated toward dogs — sled dogs. With college and other activities, she did not get into using them with sleds until Christmas 1978. Then Walt Palmer took her out with his dogs. She followed him, driving a team. She loved it. She decided to run one of his teams in the women's race in the Fur Rendezvous without having much experience. That race was a disaster for her. It made her decide she would put together her own team.

By the fall of 1979 she had assembled about 25 dogs, and she planned to run them in sprint races. Dennis Boyer suggested that her dogs looked like they would make an even better showing in the Iditarod. She followed his advice and began training for the Iditarod.

She entered the Kusko 300, prior to running the Iditarod. It was the first year of that race and weather was a

Dee Dee Jonrowe at 1984 race start. Jim Brown photo.

real problem that year. Chill factors dropped to −110 degrees. It went from −50 degrees to +40 degrees in 24 hours. Dee Dee's ultimate experience occurred in that race. Caught in the back of the pack due to the bad weather and inexperience, she became stranded. The National Guard made several attempts to locate her. Rescue teams twice had to turn back because of the conditions. Just before dark on the second day they found her. She had pretty much given up hope, and feels she probably could not have made it through another night. Although she had the proper survival gear, she suffered from hypothermia, and had lost the motivation to be able to use the things she had. She scratched. But she persevered. She entered the Iditarod race as planned.

1980 was a tough year for Iditarod mushers. A record number of mushers scratched. Her goal was to get to Nome. She found the race "really eye opening." Living along the wind-swept coast she had never driven dogs in trees, mountains, or deep snow before. She broke nine necklines between Rohn River and Farewell Lake. She was both amazed and petrified. She feels if she had had an ounce less of strength that she could not have gotten down the back side of Rainy Pass. Her sled weighed nearly 300 pounds.

By the time she reached the Yukon River she felt she was in a position to be more competitive. The temperature dropped to −20 degrees. Her dogs began to eat better. They were used to the wind and cold. She finished 24th of the 36 finishers. Twenty-six mushers did not officially complete the race.

The 1981 race provided her with an opportunity to race with Sue Firmin. The two became best of friends. Jonrowe was awarded the sportsmanship trophy for her actions that year. The ice went out on the Anvik River when they arrived there. They had to slop through the river. When she and Sue came upon Harold Ahmasuk and Frank Sampson, whose teams were sick and out of food, she turned around. Retracing the trail back to Beaver Creek checkpoint she brought food for their dogs.

Relating it now, she states that she had the dogs that were most up for the return trip. She is especially proud of her lead dog, Ruby, who willingly led her back. Ruby's name is engraved on the trophy. While those they helped ended up scratching in Unalakleet, Dee Dee Jonrowe and Sue Firmin continued on. They arrived in 31st and 32nd position, in spite of the extra 24 hours taken to help out their fellow mushers.

After taking a year off from Iditarod competition, she entered the 1983 race. It was her best year. Things went on schedule. Again she traveled with Sue Firmin. For awhile they traveled with Rick Swenson and Sonny Lindner. She learned a lot and gained much respect for them. When she arrived at Shageluk, she felt her dogs needed more rest and did not continue with her traveling companions. She rested a couple of extra hours. Then her dogs felt better and ate better.

Enroute to Unalakleet from Kaltag she was really excited. The trail was good. She hoped to catch up with the leaders. They had departed, so she pushed on. In Koyuk she caught up with Susan Butcher and Sue Firmin for breakfast. Reaching Nome in 15th position she felt really good about her dogs' performance. It was her most exciting race.

The 1984 race was her most disappointing Iditarod. Jonrowe broke three sleds that year. The brake on her sled broke before she got to Finger Lake, and the erratic sled movements were tough on her wheel dog. She dropped him at Rohn checkpoint.

Jonrowe contracted pneumonia on the trail. She spit up blood. She couldn't catch her breath. She felt she was going to suffocate. There was lots of water on the lakes. Her dogs got depressed about the water. She felt like they were only going three miles per hour. However, by the time she reached the coast she began to pick up time. Traveling with Sue Firmin, Dave Olson and Rick Mackey, they left Unalakleet at night as it was beginning to snow. Then they got caught in a bad groundstorm on the ice out of Shaktoolik. But she still managed to finish in 30th position.

After the 1984 race she sold most of her older dogs. She has been building a team of younger dogs. Many of her dogs come from Sue Firmin's bloodline. Nearly all the dogs are ones she has bred. Her main leader, Farah, came from Rick Swenson. She first used her in the 1984 season. She breeds her dogs for good feet, long back, speed and attitude. They are longer and leggier than her first dogs. A number have light coats and some may require sweaters in very cold weather. She feels their speed and other attributes are worth the extra effort and higher maintenance diet.

In 1985, Jonrowe was one of the race judges. Judges keep "leap frogging" along the trail throughout the race. For up to four weeks they get little sleep. It was stressful as she had to make decisions carefully to not give anyone a competitive edge.

She took her role seriously. She was aware of the personal investment each racer had in the race. She knew what it meant to be scared of judges, and how it felt to be a rookie. Above all she tried to be fair and to help all mushers equally.

In reflecting on what dog sled racing means to her, Jonrowe states that it has given her an identity of her own. It has opened doors to her. She does not have to prove herself. She is respected for her handling of dogs. Most of all, "I get a lot of personal pleasure working with my dogs." She can't imagine ever being without a dog. "Animals are always glad to see you and always love you."

Her dog ethics stem from her childhood. Her mother's family had a dairy farm. Her idea of the perfect summer was to spend it all on the farm. She was encouraged to appreciate animals, and to seek comfort from them when upset.

Married for eight years, her husband, Mike, is supportive of her interest in dogs. He helps feed them when she is away, although he does not participate in training them. A captain in the Bethel Fire Department, his passion is flying. Both of them do commercial gill net herring fishing in separate areas. In 1986 Jonrowe hopes to realize her dream of drift fishing commercially in Bristol Bay. While dog mushing is her passion, the fishing industry is her profession. She talks enthusiastically about both. Many of her dogs have been named for tender boats of the fishing processor she worked with recently.

Her goals encompass these two interest areas. Her first goal is to be self-employed as a Bristol Bay fisherman. Her next goals are to place in the top five in an Iditarod, and to win a dog sled race.

Jonrowe is involved year around in the Iditarod. In 1982 she helped at checkpoints as she did not race. Since 1984 she has been on the board of directors of the Iditarod Trail Committee. She sees her role as helping insure race rules are made in the best interests of all the dog drivers, and that as few roadblocks are put in front of the competitors as possible.

Jonrowe plans to run the Iditarod again. She will enter both the Kusko 300 and the John Beargrease Race in Minnesota in 1986. Since she has a real young dog team she will probably sit out the 1986 Iditarod. She plans to definitely be back on the Iditarod Trail as a race competitor by 1987.

MARJORIE MOORE

Marjorie Moore, a red-haired, artistic wood and ivory carver, traveled the trail in the 1980 Iditarod and finished 30th in a field of 62 mushers. The niece of early-Alaska bush pilot Lew Moore, she had heard tales of Alaska's interior from early childhood. She moved to Alaska in 1974 and acquired

Marjorie Moore. Jim Brown photo.

her first dog team the following year. Seeing the Rendezvous races and reading about the Iditarod inspired her "to go for it."

Her first dog team had six dogs. She learned by herself from scratch. She acquired more huskies. Several of her dogs ran to Nome in 1976 and placed 6th that year. Two years later she again loaned dogs to another musher.

Currently an Anchorage nighttime taxi driver, she has traveled extensively. She spent four years as a civil service secretary in Italy. She has also lived for short stretches in various small Alaskan villages. Woodcutter, bartender, cook, and bookkeeper are some of the many jobs she has held in Alaska.

Recounting her own trail experiences she feels it is crucial that mushers be flexible enough to respond to various situations. She never entertained the idea of scratching from the race, even though she got off the trail three times enroute to Nome. "I would have crawled over the finish line dragging the sled and carrying the dogs, if necessary!"

While discussing the moose stories of the 1985 race, Moore noted she has never had any moose encounters on the trail in spite of training near Montana Creek, an area known for its high moose population. She always used bells on her main line to warn area wildlife of her presence. Many times she has seen moose and caribou walk away from the trail having heard her coming. She borrowed this idea from old-time mail carriers, deduced from her reading about old times in Alaska.

When Moore crossed the finish line in Nome she was asked about her race. Her comment, "it was no big deal," took the questioner by surprise. The race was a positive experience for her at age 41. She also planned to enter the 1981 race. Several friends were instrumental in helping her to obtain needed sponsors. One major sponsor was ALPATCO, the air traffic controllers' union. For a number of reasons, money being the major one, she did not run in the 1981 race. Asked if she would run again the response is a big "YES, if I could get a good sponsor. I sure hate to lose all the experience I gained in those five years of training!"

During the 1980 race her dogs performed excellently. Her dogs had no problems with feet or sickness. During training she exposed them to different conditions and different kinds of food. All her dogs became "chow hounds." They loved to eat "anything and all the time." There were two times her food was not at the scheduled drop point. She and they managed to overcome that handicap by stopping at the garbage dump and "gobbling up all the many leftovers."

"The thrill is running at night with no light." She feels the dogs really enjoy being out on the trail, and the teamwork that develops is wonderful to be part of. Her team consisted of Indian River huskies with short coats. She trained 20 dogs, and usually ran them in teams of four to six dogs. Before running the Iditarod race she had only run a team of 14 dogs once or twice.

At present a city dweller, she no longer has a dog team. She still has one dog, Fox, an Iditarod veteran of three races, who quietly greets visitors at their home. Fox has "snowshoe feet" which spread out while running, a desirable quality in Iditarod dogs.

Rainy Pass was an absolutely spectacular remembrance for Marjorie. Mushing through during the day she was impressed by its sheer beauty of steep "silent granite." She also found going across the ice from Shaktoolik to Koyuk spectacular "with the curvature of the earth visible." Out on the ice when the fog came in, she had to stop and camp for the night. Flying back from Nome after the race she was surprised when she realized how close she had been to the open water.

Marjorie is impressed with the thinking capacities of huskies and their ability to recuperate under stressful conditions. In 1982, while mushing her team near Moose Pass, she broke through the ice into the main current at the bend of the river. The ice kept breaking off around her and the sled and two dogs. The other four dogs were still on the ice pulling for all they were worth, with her shouts of encouragement and the discipline that had been drilled into them. This narrow escape still brings goose bumps to her as she tells it. "It is very unnerving!" She feels fortunate to have survived that situation.

Marjorie Moore keeps busy these days working a 7-day-a-week, 12-hour-a-day job. She enjoys meeting people and talking to old-time Alaskans about their experiences. A creative person, she is writing a book on her Iditarod experience in her spare time.

BARBARA MOORE

In 1980 Barbara Moore became Nome's first female musher to compete in an Iditarod race. The former Ohio farm girl moved there in 1974 with her husband and young daughter. She remembers thinking, "Who would ever want to live in this desolate place?" Having grown up on a farm, and used to always having animals around, she soon purchased a sled dog for her daughter Lisa.

Barbara and Lisa Moore, Boots, and Red Lantern trophies. Photo courtesy of B. Moore.

With 4-year-old Lisa riding in the sled or wagon hauled by the dog, Barbara Moore started along the path of dog driving. As Lisa grew older she was right in there with mother. Now both mother and daughter race dogs. Moore came in last in 36th position, receiving the red lantern award. Five years later Lisa entered the Junior Iditarod. She also received the red lantern award in that race.

Barbara Moore remembers the best part of the Iditarod race being "seeing all the people at Nome turn out to watch me come in." She estimates that about 400 people were there to greet her on Front Street, a much larger number than usually greet the mushers at the end of the race.

Reflecting on her experience in the Iditarod, she feels she learned a lot from her traveling companion, Norman Vaughan. "He's kind of a neat companion to run with. He's always looking out for you. He's such a neat guy."

In an article entitled "The Longest Trip Home," Carol Phillips wrote about Moore's 1980 Iditarod race. Fatigued and numbed by the bone-chilling cold, Moore turned to then-75-year-old musher Norman Vaughan and said, "I'm finished, Norman; I'm scratching."[19]

> Vaughan said calmly, "You can't do that. You have to get to Farewell before you scratch."[19]

Realizing he was right she had to continue. There were only 20 miles more. Reaching Farewell, she was welcomed with hot food, friendly faces, a good night's sleep and a refreshing shower. By the next morning she felt much better. She was rested. Her dogs were feeling better. In spite of reports of a rough trail from Farewell to Nikolai, she decided to continue.

Countless times on the trail the agony of loneliness, of feeling lost and abandoned broke through. By traveling in fairly close proximity to Vaughan and musher Landon Carter (who, although disqualified early in the race, continued to Nome as he was traveling to raise funds for World Hunger), their good humor and wide knowledge helped raise her spirits and keep her in the race.

Her dogs performed well. She spent many hours caring for them, "booting" them up where needed. They were full of vitality due to her meticulous care and well planned dog diet.

She was less fortunate. Her feet suffered from the cold in spite of bunny boots. As she headed toward Galena she lost sight of her traveling companions and felt hopelessly lost. She felt terrible. Making it safely into Galena, she was greeted with the cheery news that there were messages for her.

To her delight there were many messages and more than a dozen bags of cookies from friends and family in Nome. As she progressed along the trail messages greeted her at all checkpoints. Their effect on her morale was astounding. At Unalakleet she received a portable radio from her mother, allowing her to tune in to happenings in the world and in the Iditarod. Being at the end of the pack, some checkpoints lacked veterinarians or officials when she arrived.[20]

But not everyone had forgotten the tail end mushers. Messages continued to greet her in each village. By Shaktoolik Barbara was firmly convinced she was going to make it to Nome.

Running along behind her sled she paid scant attention to the plane circling overhead between Golovin and White Mountain. Then the plane passed by low and dropped a paper sack. Retrieving it she was delighted to find it contained egg salad sandwiches on homemade bread and a note encouraging her to keep going. Then it dawned on her that husband Gary was up there in friend Mike Buckle's airplane. Her spirits uplifted, her batteries were recharged as her adrenalin surged.

Her team surged forward, and they sped ahead. As high winds made the trail hard to follow on Topkok Hill, Moore sailed along comfortably. She was now in home territory. She knew her way. The miles ticked away quickly.

Outside of Safety, the last checkpoint, she was greeted by her own personal welcoming committee — her mother and father, and at least 15 other relatives had snowmachined the 22 miles to greet her. Buoyed by this welcome the last miles sped by quickly. In Nome mushing down Front Street to the arched finish line, she was engulfed by the magnitude of her fellow townspeople's welcome.[21]

Since that momentous occasion, Barbara has experienced many new experiences. Her marriage fell apart. She left Nome in 1981 to ease the pain of divorce, settling in Florida to get as far away from Nome as possible. She disliked Florida. In 1982 she returned to Nome. Before she left Nome she sold all her dogs but three of her leaders: Boots, Digger and Duke, whom she left in California. She brought them back to Nome and began rebuilding her team. Digger has since died from a bee sting and Duke died this spring at age 14.

Boots is the only dog she has left from her 1980 Iditarod team. At 12 Boots is now retired from racing chores, although he led daughter Lisa's 1985 Junior Iditarod team. Her dogs are mostly young dogs, 2 years old, except for a couple 7 years old and younger. She has a litter of pups. Once the pups get old enough they will form daughter Lisa's team. Lisa is into speed and mother is into a steady, controllable team.

Working recently as a heavy equipment operator hauling rock on the Council Road, Barbara Moore has a diversity of work experience. Prior to her current occupation, she worked for three years as Nome's substance abuse counselor. She has worked as a deck hand on a tug boat and as a secretary, but has never used the computer keypunch skills for which she attended trade school after high school graduation.

Barbara Moore runs the dog races in her area. Her highest finish came in the David Walluk race where she placed 4th of 18 entrants. She is proud of her record of only one race scratch. That scratch came in the 1984 Nome Sweepstakes race to Fantasy Island. One and a half days into the race she was caught in a storm. After much agonizing she was forced to drop out.

Barbara Moore's goals at present include going to school to become a veterinary assistant and having a team that will allow her to compete in the top four in a race. The latter is a bit complicated by her attempts to keep the size of her dog lot small. She is currently breeding her own dogs. They come from dogs owned by Joe Redington Sr., Issac Okleasik, Susan Butcher, Sonny Lindner and Rick Swenson.

She has two daughters, Lisa and Carla. Carla, her younger daughter, is the opposite of Lisa, the musher. Carla enjoys being indoors, playing with her Cabbage Patch dolls, and dancing. Although she is not presently interested in sled dog racing herself, she attends races and cheers on both her mother and sister. She also helps feed the dogs and plays with the puppies. She has her own dog, Jules.

Moore feels the Iditarod taught her 10 years worth of dog mushing. She is glad she entered it. She hasn't decided whether she would like to run it again, although she would like to place higher than last position. She feels every race she runs is a new challenge, and she always learns something new. She dislikes the starts of races as her nervous stomach always gives her fits. There is "a little bit of competitiveness" in her. Her daughter Lisa's staunch support has egged her on to higher attainments as she knows she will have to put up with Lisa's comments if she gets bored and falters. Admiringly, she states, "Lisa is kind of teaching me."

Lisa Moore has a profound influence on her mother's racing career. In fact, one of Lisa's goals is to race in the Iditarod race when she turns 18. She wants her mother to race in that race with her. If she succeeds, it may be the first time a mother and daughter team have run in the Iditarod.

Mushing along the coastal ice. Jim Brown photo.

Sue Firmin along the trail. Jim Brown photo.

CHAPTER 5

New Women Entrants: 1981-1983

Three women again placed in the money in 1981. Susan Butcher placed 5th for the second year in a row. Donna Gentry placed 18th and Libby Riddles finished in 20th position. Sue Firmin placed 32nd in her first of several years competing in the Iditarod.

1982 was a banner year for Susan Butcher. (See chapter 4.) She placed second in the race. By now her race record matched that of almost any race competitor, except for Rick Swenson, for consistent top finishing position in races entered. Swenson's record of four Iditarod Race victories puts him in a class by himself.

Only three women entered the race in 1982. Of these women only Susan Butcher placed in the top twenty finishers. Rookie musher Rose Albert finished 32nd.

Ten women entered the 1983 race. Nine of them completed it to Nome. Seven of these women were rookies, racing for the first time in the Iditarod. The 68 mushers who left the Anchorage starting line that year for Nome were the largest number of mushers who had entered the race.

SUE FIRMIN

Sue Firmin, a lifelong Alaskan, first ran a dog team when she was nine years old. Living in the Sand Lake-Jewel Lake Road area of Anchorage, a neighbor had dogs that belonged to Earl Norris. She and her brother Tom helped care for the dogs. They also ran teams with three dogs. When the neighbor moved out of state, Earl Norris gave Sue and her brother five of the dogs. She continued to run the dogs until her senior year of high school.

"I guess running dogs is something that once you've done it . . . its always in your blood."

Several years later: "I got an old husky out of the dog pound and had an old harness . . . (I) found the old sled my brother and I made . . . . It was all beat up and weathered. I put the old dog on the sled and away we went. And I just knew that I had to get some more. When you get two or three that's not enough. You've got to have five. And then that's not enough. And pretty soon you end up with lots of dogs."

From 1972 to 1976 she spent her winters in Fort Yukon where she and her husband, Bill, ran a trapline. They only kept seven or eight dogs because everything had to be flown in. Everything they took had to fit in the 206 plane they hired to haul their gear or in Bill's PA 12.

"In the fall of 1980 I decided I had to run the Iditarod. I had been watching the Iditarod since it started and I had always

Sue Firmin at 1983 race start. Jim Brown photo.

wanted to run it. . . . In '80 I told my husband I wanted to run the Iditarod that winter and we just had to quit talking about it and do it. He kind of laughed. And then pretty soon he realized that I wasn't kidding him. We didn't know beans about what we were getting into — training and all that. Basically my team in '81 was all young dogs. Half the team was year-and-a-half-old dogs.

"At first it was a challenge. I personally wanted to see if I could do it. I was only going to run it one time. But once I ran it I knew I should have done better. That I could do better. Of course, then I had to go back . . . . There's something about the Iditarod that just pulls you back every year. So for four years I kept running."

Firmin took off 1985 and had planned to run in 1986. In May 1985 she had knee surgery, necessitated by an injury at age 12 that continued to plague her. As of November 1985 her knee was still not strong enough so she plans to sit out the 1986 Iditarod. She had more problems than usual with her knee in the 1985 KUSKO 300. She ended up riding the runners into Bethel as she couldn't use her knee. Looking back she says there is no way she could have run the 1985 Iditarod.

"I don't want to run the Iditarod again just to run it . . . I've seen the trail four times, and I don't just want to see the trail again. I want to go because I want to do well. I want to improve on my 14th place finish. I know I should be able to do it. I've got the dogs to do it."

Firmin feels she has learned a lot from the race.

"In terms of the dogs I've learned a lot about feeding and caring for the dogs on the race. Obviously every year you go you learn something else. As far as running the race, that's the most important thing. It's time saving things and how to care for and feed the dogs. That right there is the whole race. That's where a rookie is at a disadvantage."

Firmin likes the race for the people and for being able to be out with the dogs. She likes spending 24 hours a day with her dogs. She always takes a camera as she enjoys seeing the country.

"What better way to see the land! I've met so many wonderful people on the trail. I've made some fantastic friends through the Iditarod . . . . A lot of them are our closest friends now. Just the people out there is the biggest thing. The volunteers out there and the people I've stayed with. It's just unbelievable how they open their house up and have me in and feed you. They're just wonderful. That's probably the neatest thing about the race.

" '81 was my first year. That's the year I met Dee Dee (Jonrowe). Of course, we're the best of buddies now.

" '83 was a good year. The weather was good. I felt good. The dogs felt good. Everything went great. That was the year I finished 14th.

" '84 it seemed every time we got up something would knock us down. So we decided we would just finish, and that's what we did.

"To win that race or to do good you have to have a lot of luck, and everything has got to go right. You have to have no sick dogs. You've got to plan everything and have no problems . . . . It's hard to go for two or three weeks — whatever it takes — with say 15 dogs, and you're heading out into Alaskan weather and have absolutely everything go perfect . . . . It's kind of a gamble. And it's an expensive gamble."

She estimates it costs her about $20,000 to run the race. She owns all her own dogs. She doesn't lease any. Her husband makes her sleds. Her biggest expense is for dog food. She feeds her dogs a high grade commercial dog food plus various types of meat year around. Every year new equipment like harnesses, new lines, etc. is needed. There are airplane tickets for her and the dogs.

"I'll pay my last Iditarod bill in June. Then I'll sign up in July, and it starts all over again. It's a year around cost and a year around job."

She plans to run the Iditarod at least once more. She will probably stay in mid-distance racing longer. Sue lives all the time at Flat Horn Lake where she does her training. Husband Bill is very supportive of her racing. He works seasonally in Anchorage. By Thanksgiving or Christmas he is back full time at Flat Horn Lake. He repairs her equipment and cuts trails for her. While working in Anchorage he commutes in his own plane to the lake. Sometimes he helps her with training. She notes appreciatively, "Without his help I couldn't race." Sometimes he meets her at trail checkpoints giving her encouragement.

Sue's eight-year-old daughter, Teresa, is supportive also. She helped sponsor her mother in the 1985 KUSKO 300, paying air fare for both of them to the race. Sometimes she is less enthusiastic. From the time she was six months old until a couple of years ago, she was bundled up in the sled during many training runs, giving her a unique outlook on the situation.

Her parents, Stan and Jane Wilk, have also been supportive. Many times when she thought she couldn't go on she'd receive a message from them that gave her renewed energy. After scratching from the race in 1982 they met her in Nome. This was very important to her. She feels making the decision to scratch was probably the hardest decision she ever made because she doesn't like to quit anything.

Firmin's first dogs were the larger malemute type used on their Fort Yukon area trapline. These were slower than her present dogs. The "Sue Firmin breed" has a lot of Siberian husky. Some have a trace of wolf. All are her version of the "Alaskan racing husky," a dog bred for speed and toughness. Some of her dogs have a short fur coat, a disadvantage in extreme cold. She put dog sweaters on them in some races. On the other hand, her dogs are ideal in warmer weather. Her dogs are fast, and can trot 30 miles in less than 2½ hours.

Joel Kottke is her encyclopedia for information. When she has questions she goes to talk with him. "He is a philosopher of dog mushing." (Kottke has been active in the Iditarod Race since the 1967 race, and completed the trip to Nome as a racer in 1974.) It was from Joel that she purchased Peggy, her old leader, who is the "foundation to all my dogs." Kottke has played an important part in her training and racing.

Sue Firmin served on the Iditarod Trail Board of Directors from 1983 to 1985, volunteering her knowledge as a musher and resident near the Iditarod Trail. The Board decisions have not always been ones with which she has agreed, but her voice and wisdom have been heard. She hopes her influence has helped make the race viable and the board aware of the views of residents along the trail impacted by the race.

For many top Iditarod mushers, dog mushing is a profession. For Firmin it is a hobby that "is nice to make money if I can." Her lifestyle is a bush lifestyle in which dogs have a prominent place. She wants to improve on her 1983 14th place finish.

She knows she has dogs that can finish as race winners. Firmin candidly admits she could never win the race because her priorities as a mother and family person mean she is unlikely to commit the needed time and resources to training. Yet she has the faith and confidence in herself to see what she and her dogs can do the next time. And when she does run again she will be living the challenge the race means to her.

ROSE ALBERT

Rose Albert, an Athabascan Indian from Ruby, has the distinction of being the first Alaska Native woman to compete in the Iditarod. She entered in 1982. She proudly points to her family history of successful dog team racers. Her grandmother, Alice Albert, was a consistent winner in the women's race in Kokrines, Alaska, in the early years. Her late brother, Howard Albert, compiled an impressive list of racing accomplishments, and successfully placed in the money in the four Iditarod races he entered.

Reflecting on her interest in dogs and dog teams she remembers growing up around dogs. Her family always had dogs until snowmachines started becoming popular.

"Everyone gave up their dogs for a time until this Iditarod race started. Now dogs are all back."

She credits her brother Howard with training her and teaching her how to handle a dog team. When she decided to enter the race he let her use twelve of his dogs. She readily admits her inexperience as she describes her early experiences in training. Remembering training as the "funnest part," she had the luxury of five months to seriously prepare for the Iditarod. When she headed out into rugged country about 40 miles southeast of Ruby to train, Howard had her drive the team out by herself. Reminiscing about that trip she described her experience on the narrow trail.

"I went heading down the trail on a steep hill between the trees. First thing I did was crash into a tree. I broke up the bumper on the sled, Howard's $600 sled. I managed to pick up the dogs. They were so anxious cause they knew Howard was up ahead on the snow machine. I got the sled out. Crashing down into a creek, on a narrow winding trail up the creek . . . I lost my scarf. A tree grabbed it or something . . . . Farther down the trail . . . I broke up the runners . . ."

Looking back she realizes the dogs were ready to run. It was she that needed to get ready. She continued to shave more trees on the trail. After a number of weeks learning how to handle the dogs, the day came to head back to Ruby.

"Howard said, 'Do you think you can make it back by yourself?' . . . I headed back to Ruby . . . I got lost in a real deep creek. It was raining out and everything was turning to ice. He said he made a new trail. 'You should have no problem.' Well, sure enough I went flying down that trail. I crashed into a tree . . . broke up my sled. I chained it together and tied it together with rope and everything. Got to the bottom of the hill. Two things fell out of the bottom of my sled. Walked back up the hill, picked up what I lost and I went back to the top of the cliff and the dogs were gone. They went about four miles down the creek, and they crashed into a big log sticking out. That's how they stopped. So I took off my rope and my axe and I just tied my sled together."

After that experience she decided to let Pepper, her lead dog, go where she wanted to go and Pepper found the trail. They were able to get back to Ruby without too much trouble.

"I got to Ruby. It was pitch dark. I was soaking wet and so were my dogs . . . . I went into the house . . . my dad got a flashlight and went outside."

After looking over her sled, he shook his head and said:

"Rose how did you make it in with *that*?? How did you make it back with that?" He also asked me if my head was warm. My marten hat was caked over with ice from the rain, like a helmet.

Rose's father, Phillip Albert Sr., who made all of Howard's sleds then, asked her older brother George to make her a sled that wouldn't break. George made her a very heavy birch sled. He made it well. She didn't break it. But it was extremely heavy which caused problems of a different kind. Describing them she relates the difficulty she had going up to Happy.

"I came to this steep hill. And from the sun there wouldn't be any snow. Just mud. And I can't push my dogs up the hill because my sled was too heavy. And the dogs would pull as hard as they could but the sled wouldn't move on the mountain. So I'd have to carry everything up the hill out of my sled and then push my dogs up. Then put everything back on the sled and then take off."

Rose has many wonderful memories of her first Iditarod. She views it as a learning experience and would like to enter again. She had plans for entering the 1985 race, in memory of her brothers Howard and Harvey, and had lined up some sponsors. However, the promised money never arrived and she had to change her mind.

The problem of sponsorship is one all mushers face. She remembers her brother Howard as being pretty independent and not relying heavily on sponsors. He was an excellent trapper and raised much of his own expense money. She had worked on the Slope at one time and helped him financially.

When she decided to run in the 1985 race, Andy Folger and his father were a tremendous support to her as they had been to Howard during his racing career. Andy Folger was going

Rose Albert. R. Nielsen photo.

to lease her six of his dogs. She had five of her own she planned to take. Soon after making the decision not to compete in 1985 she moved from Ruby to Anchorage. In Anchorage she does not have a team. But she has dreams of again racing at a later date.

Rose started in the 1982 Iditarod race with 12 dogs. When she arrived in Nome 20 days later she had eleven of her original dogs. She had been forced to drop only one. Rae Rae, an all-white dog, had slipped on the ice enroute to Rohn River and broke her leg. It was so icy that Rose was not able to put her brake in the snow to stop the team. She managed to take the dog out of harness in less than a minute's time, wrap her leg in a splint while the dogs were still running, and put her in her sled. Needed surgery to repair her injuries was quite expensive. The veterinarian's receptionist fell in love with Rae Rae and agreed to pay for the surgery if she could keep her. Thus, Rae Rae retired from the racing circuit and lives in sunny California.

Rose Albert quickly informs you about how her late brother Howard taught her most of what she knows about dogs. Howard believed in feeding his dogs well year around. He cooked food for them year around. For the race the dogs were fed lots of beaver for quick energy. Her father cut up chunks of beaver that her brothers had trapped. This was fed to each dog at each checkpoint. There were beef burgers, a high quality commercial dog food, lots of liver, and frozen fish cooked with rice or oats or corn meal. Howard taught her how to recognize foot problems and how to care for the dog's feet to prevent potential problems.

She is especially proud of Howard's lead dog Pepper. Pepper was nine at the time of the race. Her swing dogs were faster than Pepper and at times almost ran over him. She tried various combinations of the other dogs in lead but never really developed another strong leader. "Pepper could read a blind trail." And he did for Rose.

Rose was very impressed with the way she was treated by village people along the trail, remarking they treated her "so wonderful." At almost every checkpoint the women would wait for her to come in. She went through villages she thought she would never see, and liked them all.

Just because she was competing in a race did not make Rose compromise her rest or her personal appearance. She feels she would have done much better if she had rested less. She made sure she received eight or more hours of sleep most of the time. If she didn't feel like going she didn't. She knew she had good dogs and that they were fast. The dogs performed well. They never gave her any problems and they never got sick. She remembers one night, as they neared the end of the race, where she and several mushers got stranded near Topkok Hill.

"It got so cold. The chill factor was so bad all our headlamps went out and we couldn't see.... I had these otter mitts that belonged to my father I didn't want to lose.... I dropped one so I parked my dogs and I walked all over that hill till I found the mitt.... Then we couldn't find the trail back. We found it cause we ran smack into some dog musher that was sleeping on the trail...."

"We were all lost. There were five of us.... We went blasting down that mountain in the morning at the crack of dawn."

When they arrived at the next checkpoint, Rose went inside to brush her hair and put on her Oil of Olay and get something warm to drink. When she went back out the others had left. They didn't want her to beat them to Nome. So she stayed and fed her dogs. She still had hopes of catching up with them anyway.

Rose's brother Howard used some of the same dogs the next year when he again entered the Iditarod.

In August 1983 Howard died. Rose had been planning to leave Ruby a few days later to go to school to work on her bachelor's degree. She stayed to tend the family business.

About six months later two of her brothers had another tragedy. Out on their trapline the weather changed, and they suffered from hypothermia. By the time they were rescued, one died and the other suffered loss of both feet and his fingers. It was a very painful time for Rose.

That summer and fall she debated about her future. When her plans to run the 1985 Iditarod were stymied she decided to leave Ruby. She moved to Anchorage. Before leaving Ruby she sold the dogs and most of their equipment. However, she misses her dogs.

Rose Albert is a talented artist. A graduate of the Institute of American Indian Arts in Santa Fe, New Mexico, she paints portraits of people she has known and scenes that reflect the traditional village way of life. She views herself as a modern, contemporary artist, however. Someday she hopes to return to Ruby with her own family and be able to have a team and again race dogs.

For now she is content with expanding her horizons and painting scenes that reflect her cultural tradition. One of her oil paintings, "A Frosty Morning on the Iditarod Trail," is reproduced on the front cover of this book.

ROXY WRIGHT

Roxy Wright is a famous sprint racer who entered the 1983 Iditarod as a rookie Iditarod racer. The winner, at that time, of seven Anchorage Women's World Championships, many Fairbanks Women's North American Championships and a successful competitor in the Fairbanks Open North American Championship and the Anchorage World Championship Sled Dog Races, she had built a reputation as one of Alaska's most successful sprint racers.

She decided to enter the Iditarod because it was something she personally wanted to do. As the time drew closer to the Iditarod, she decided she wanted to run in the Anchorage Fur Rendezvous races as well, so she took

Roxy Wright. Jim Brown photo.

some weight off the dogs to speed them up. She placed fourth in the women's race. In the Open World Championship race she placed sixth. Then with less than two weeks to go to the start of the Iditarod she tried to fatten up her dogs and "slow them down again."

Wright firmly believes that the same dogs can run either sprint or long distance races. The main difference is in the way the dogs are trained. They also need to think differently. She feels her dogs would have done much better in the Iditarod if she knew what she was doing. She feels she made a lot of mistakes, but was happy with how her dogs did.

She really respects and enjoyed the Iditarod. She equally, if not more, enjoys and respects sprint racing. Reflecting on her Iditarod experience, she remembers enjoying the different kinds of countryside she traveled through. In contrast to sprint racing the Iditarod was a different pace. Sprint racing does not allow much time to focus on the scenery. Speed is important, making what the dogs are doing significant every single moment. In the Iditarod the dogs need to pace themselves. This puts less pressure on both dogs and musher, allowing the musher to often be more relaxed. She enjoyed the differences in training, especially in being able to have a more relaxed pace with her dogs. She placed in 23rd position.

Although she enjoyed running the Iditarod she does not plan to do it again in the near future. Being a mother of teenagers, she feels the kind of training required in preparation for sprint races is easier on family life. She feels she did not get enough experience prior to the Iditarod in camping training trips with her dogs. That experience is one she feels is needed to help dogs think in the different way that is needed in a long distance race such as the Iditarod. She feels it took her dogs a week on the Iditarod Trail to get settled and figure things out. If she decides to compete in the Iditarod again, she feels it would be best to spend a couple of years of training her dogs for long distance mushing.

Although she is definitely a serious sprint dog racer, Wright does not consider dogs her whole life. Being the daughter of Gareth Wright, well-known Alaskan sprint racer, she has been exposed to dogs and dog racing most of her life. She is one of eight daughters. One of her younger sisters, Lynette Hughes, has also raced. Her youngest sister, Shannon Earhart, will be running in her first Anchorage Women's World Championship Race in 1986. Shannon has also raced in junior races.

At age 16 Roxy Wright began her successful racing career. Eighteen years later she says she does not believe her children will get into serious racing. She would like to see them attend college. Although she has not formally attended college she has taken a few courses. She would like to take additional ones. She has lots of hobbies and interests, but being busy with the dogs leaves her little time to pursue some of them. She would like to do more sewing and art work. Sailing is another hobby. Recently she has managed to fit in some summer sailing trips.

In spite of her remarkable success as a sprint racer, it has not always been particularly financially lucrative for her. Sprint races tend to have small purses. Weather impacts on earnings. Bad weather (such as poor snow conditions) can cause cancellations of major races, dashing hopes for winning money. There is tremendous competition for sponsors. The advent of the Iditarod and other long distance races means more mushers are looking for sponsors. Dillingham Corporation has been a really good sponsor for Wright the past couple of years. Due to corporate changes they will no longer be able to sponsor her.

Today Roxy Wright has a dog lot in partnership with veteran musher Charlie Champaine. In the fall of 1985 they were training 50 dogs. These will be reduced to 30 dogs in preparation for the winter racing season. Her dogs are a special breed, developed under the guidance of her father, with additions of dogs from other mushers. Her father's breed is known as the Aurora husky or Gareth Wright hound. These dogs are less than one-quarter Irish setter and a three-quarters mix of the Alaskan husky breed. She has purchased dogs from Iditarod mushers as well as sold dogs to Iditarod mushers.

SHANNON CHASE POOLE

Shannon Chase Poole, artist and sculptor, took to the trail as one of 68 racers in the 1983 Iditarod. She finished in 29th position. A talented, energetic person, Shannon has a love for animals which is shown in her watercolor paintings.

The Pooles live on fourteen acres in Trapper Creek, Alaska, with two lakes. They have built their own home. It is surrounded by windows facing a lake on one side and her dog lot on the other side. Their rustic home, filled with her art, antiques, and prisms, captures the sunlight. Its airy feeling immediately puts visitors at ease. Her Maine coon cat lies inside on an oriental rug while horses graze outside near sled dogs.

During the race she took her camera with intentions of photographing

Shannon Chase Poole. R. Nielsen photo.

Bred for speed, some are really fast dogs.

Shannon hopes to enter the 1986 Iditarod. Her decision to do so or not will be partially based on her success in attracting sponsors.

Thirty-eight dogs occupied her dog lot in October 1985. She cares for them by herself. Having her size dog lot is definitely a "tie down" proposition. "Nobody takes care of them the same way you do." She tries to keep the dogs on a schedule, feeding them the same time each day. Each dog has the opportunity to run free for part of each day. Having raised each dog from birth, each knows to come when she says "come." She can place

the countryside. She sought inspiration for future artwork. The cold made fingers sluggish and kept her from taking many photographs. She remembers feeling so cold she wondered aloud, "What are you doing out here?" She discovered her clothing was inadequate for the intense cold.

Among her memories she thinks back to a "real neat spot" — going across the ice from Shaktoolik. It was a clear, cold night. The northern lights put on an incredible display. Traveling in the stillness of night the lights of Koyuk were visible for hours. Twinkling in the distance they seemed a large number. It was like a mirage. When she arrived she was shocked by how few lights there actually were there.

The biggest problem her dogs had during the race was boredom. She moved them to different positions in the team. They felt that was great, and their pace and interest picked up immediately.

Shannon and husband Eric Poole raise all their own dogs. The dogs she raced with are descendants of dogs which Eric's brother, Jim Teegarden, acquired when he started sprint racing in the late 1960s. Eric purchased his team a few years later. The original dogs came from Gareth Wright, George Attla and Dennis Crisman.

Pen and ink drawing by Shannon Chase Poole © 1982. Used with permission of Shannon Chase Poole.

"Rainy Pass," watercolor by Shannon Chase Poole © 1983. Used with permission of Shannon Chase Poole.

harnesses on them, let them run loose while harnessing up others, and have each dog come on command. She is a strict disciplinarian and is very consistent in her training program.

Shannon loves her dogs very much. Yet at times she feels so tied down by them that she has considered selling all but a few of them. She feels it would be great to have just enough dogs to form one dog team. Then she would be free to drive off on overnight trips to her cabin, twenty miles away. She would not need to hire someone to feed the rest of her dogs as none would be left behind.

Sharing the area near her dogs are two draft horses, Mack and Mark, that Eric recently purchased. She also has her pet horse. Summers, she maintains a large garden. Blooming plants hang under the roof overhang. All these activities leave limited time to pursue her artwork.

Mainly known for her wildlife watercolors, she has recently taken up sculpture. A six-inch-high sculpture in exquisite detail of a wolf, and a more stylized one of a musk ox done in bronze, herald her entry into this new medium of artistic expression. She finds doing sculptures "really fun." Working with modeling compound in three dimensional form comes easier than trying to express the three dimensions in one dimensional form.

She is one of three children, and her parents are antique dealers in Minnesota. All the children live in Alaska. Her sister, an M.D., has recently joined a medical practice in Anchorage.

Shannon has always been an animal lover. As a youngster the family had a German shepherd. She had a cart for him. "He just loved pulling it." In high school she had her own horse. She also trained horses. She attended college for three years, with the goal of becoming a veterinarian. She came to Alaska after her junior year and has never left.

Shannon's husband ran the Iditarod race in 1980, and placed 31st of 62 entrants. Now Shannon is the one who is involved in the care and training of the family dog team. She has indeed found a new life for herself with her artistic talents and love of animals among the pristine beauty of Alaska's rugged countryside.

CHRIS O'GAR

Chris O'Gar, a native of Shelter Island, New York, and Alaskan resident since she graduated from high school in 1977, entered the 1983 Iditarod. She placed 32nd out of 68 entrants. The then 23-year-old musher became interested in the race because she kept "running into people who ran the race."

She was hired by Duane Halverson, Iditarod race veteran, as a dog handler. She then knew she "wanted to get into dogs." The next year she put together a team. It included four dogs of her own, six she leased from Halverson, and six more leased dogs. Her love of dogs has never diminished. In the fall of 1985 she and a partner have a dog lot with about 80 dogs.

That 1983 race experience is "something I'll always remember." She feels she learned a lot. "The whole experience was a great mixture of mental and physical exertion." It was fun being out there with the dogs. Just knowing she could travel that far with her dogs meant a lot, as did seeing the real teamwork that is necessary in an endeavor of the magnitude of the Iditarod race.

She remembers being lost twice, which cost her 24 hours altogether. She had never really traveled the trail before, as her only trip along the trail had been on the section from the Matanuska Valley to Skwentna. In 1981 she trained with Duane Halverson. In 1982 in preparation for the race she trained by herself.

Since 1983 she has been breeding her own dogs. They are a "kickoff" from Halverson's breed, and are a mixture of husky and hound. The

Christine O'Gar. Photo courtesy of Christine O'Gar.

dogs average 45 to 50 pounds. She now feels she has a handful of good dogs. Her emphasis now is on middle distance racing. Some of her dogs last year ran in the Coldfoot Classic race as part of Rusty Miller's team. She ran in the Bull's Eye to Angel Creek Race, and was the top female placer in the race in eighth position.

The issue of money for long distance racing inevitably clouds the picture of Chris' own hopes for the future. She plans to run in either the Iditarod or the Yukon Quest Race in the next couple of years. Having done the Iditarod once successfully, she wants to do it again and do better. She estimates it cost her close to $20,000 to run the Iditarod.

Since moving to Alaska in 1977 she has spent a number of summers commercial fishing and cooking in the Kotzebue area. For a time she lived year around in that area. She used her dogs for both transportation and pleasure. The summer of 1985 was the first summer she did not work out of Kotzebue. She moved to Fairbanks where she is partner in a good dog lot. Fairbanks is a contrast to her village experience of tents, fish and camping, and she hopes this new location will allow her better access to middle distance races.

When talking with Chris one gets

caught up in her enthusiasm. Her life revolves around dogs and racing.

Having come to Alaska after being infected with Alaska fever by a friend who raved and raved about the country, she has adopted it. Her goal is the goal so many seek. To live her life the way she loves, with her dogs and enjoying the solitude of the trail, as well as the companionship of both human and animal friends.

This is a far cry from Long Island, New York, where she grew up the second of three girls born to Marion and Henry O'Gar. There this very outdoors oriented individual owned horses and went sailing and swimming. Now she cooks over a wood stove and has a large fish pot. The surroundings have changed. The love of animals and the outdoors hasn't.

CONNIE FRERICHS

Connie Frerichs of Delta Junction has participated twice in the Iditarod Race (1983 and 1984). She also entered the Yukon Quest race in 1985.

After the Frerichs moved to Alaska in 1975, Connie felt the need for something more to do. Her husband was gone a lot working on the North Slope. In Minnesota, their former home, the Frerichs had raised German shepherds. So she took up sled dog racing. Her kennel now has about 50 dogs — Alaskan husky and a mixture of "everything."

In 1978 she attended the local races. Mushers in her area hold get togethers every week or every other week in the winter. It is a good way to take the dogs out and everyone has a good time.

Looking back at her Iditarod experience she recalls it being "a great experience." She enjoyed getting to see the villages. "It's a great feeling" to have accomplished her goal of getting to Nome.

Contrasting her Yukon Quest participation to the Iditarod race, she notes that in the Quest you can't take as many dogs because you are only allowed to drop three dogs during the entire race. Therefore, the dogs have to carry more weight as there are some large distances between checkpoints. At one point her dogs had to haul 300 pounds. The training for the two races is somewhat different. She feels you really have to know your dogs. There are lots of hills in the Quest. The dogs go slow up the hills which often are two to three miles in length.

She learned about dog mushing through reading books and by helping Sonny Lindner pack food one year. She also mushed some with him. It was through her working with Sonny Lindner, in helping with his preparations for an Iditarod Race, that she became interested in the Iditarod.

She has a number of lead dogs. One, Ring, went to Nome with Lindner in 1979. At that time he was not a lead dog. When she obtained him she trained him as a leader. Now a nine-year-old, Ring has the role of teaching pups. He was hit by a buffalo while in training for the Quest one time when her husband had him out on the trail. Frerichs is proud of Ring whom she refers to as a "good old boy." On the 1983 Iditarod, while struggling to find her way on the ice between Shaktoolik and Koyuk, she let Ring have his way and he found the trail. He successfully located the markers and led her to Koyuk.

Currently she has five main lead dogs — Spook, Penny, Jangles, Nickel and Dodger. Dodger, a very attractive dog, constantly attracts comments from mushers. When the guys would say, "I like your dog," Dodge would reply, "Ruff, Ruff." Then he would become very protective of her. Prior to the race his protectiveness was something she had never observed. Dodge also went to Nome as a member of Lindner's 1979 team. Again, it was Connie who trained Dodge to be a leader.

Reflecting on the 1983 Iditarod, Frerichs feels the race went pretty smoothly. The weather was decent. (Although that year was a fairly cold one on the trail, being from the cold Interior of Alaska she is used to very cold temperatures.) She enjoyed seeing all the villages. Her only time of being really lost was enroute to Nikolai. She had headlight problems. It was at night. She knew she was close by, but stopped on the ice. There she awaited daylight so she could see the markers. The only other major snag for her was her stove. "It just didn't work the way it was supposed to work." She arrived in Nome in about 17½ days in 39th position.

In 1984 she had a team with a lot of young dogs. There was a lot of open water that year on the lakes.

Connie Frerichs and husband Jim. Note license plate "MUSHON." Photo courtesy of C. Frerichs.

The dogs would punch through the crust into two or three feet of water and go under. She had difficulty trying to keep her sled up above the slush. Everyone got wet. She didn't want to burn her team out. Since there was no hope of getting up front, and for safety considerations, she ended up scratching at McGrath.

In 1985 she had a successful experience in the Yukon Quest International Sled Dog Race from Whitehorse, Yukon Territory, Canada, to Fairbanks, Alaska. One of five female entrants, she placed 19th of the 34 racers who started, arriving in thirteen plus days.

Connie Frerichs was raised on a farm in Minnesota. There were always lots of animals. However, she always had to share the family dogs. The second of four children, she is the only one who has been to Alaska. However, her parents are quite interested in her sled dog racing experiences as are some of her other family members. As an outgrowth of her farm upbringing, she maintains a large garden and lots of animals. These include many rabbits and six sheep as well as lambs.

The mother of two teenagers, ages 17 and 15, she is a full-time dog trainer and homemaker. Her children have their own interests, but do help out some with her activities. Her husband is employed by Atlantic Richfield at Prudhoe Bay. His schedule is one week on and one week off. He has been very supportive of her sled dog activities. He helps her train the dogs as well as care for them. Generally they have at least two dog teams. She has about 50 dogs. They eat about 100 pounds of dog food a day, at a cost of about $300 a month. Neighbors and friends sewed the many dog booties she used on the Iditarod.

Connie Frerichs is justifiably proud of two dogs she saved from certain death. Rocky and Jessie, half Saint Bernard and half McKenzie River husky, are well known for their weight pulling feats. Each has won two championships at the Anchorage Fur Rondy weight pulling contest.

Frerichs is considering participating in the 1986 Yukon Quest Race. She likes middle and long distance racing better than sprint racing. She feels you get to know your dogs better, and you are able to race your dogs for more years than you can in sprint races.

FRITZ KIRSCH

"Fritz" Kirsch's introduction to the world of dog mushing came from Lolly Medley, Iditarod race pioneer. At the time Fritz was working at the University Dairy Farm Research Center in Palmer. One day at the local feed store she and Lolly were talking. Lolly's friend, Gene Leonard of Rainy Pass, needed help in getting his dog food packed for the race. Fritz decided to help him. Lolly laid out the formula for what he wanted sent to each checkpoint.

> "Lolly said, 'Why don't you come over?' So I went over and she hooked up three dogs. So that's basically how I got started."

Kirsch then volunteered at the Iditarod headquarters, doing a lot of paperwork. Later she worked for various female mushers including Varona Thompson. She moved on to having a couple of fun teams of her own. In 1981:

> "I was up at Iditarod one day and in pops Joe (Redington) Sr. I talked with him a little while. I went out and worked for him and his kennels for about a year and a half. Then I worked out a situation where I was allowed to use some of his dogs. And that was the beginning. Basically that's where all my breed stock comes from — Knik Kennels."

She now has about forty dogs at her own kennel. When she entered the Iditarod in 1983 she leased some dogs from Joe Redington Sr's kennel. A few dogs were her own dogs. Kirsch estimates it cost her $15,000 to $20,000 plus lost wages when she was in training and on the trail for her 1983 race experience.

Fritz Kirsch. Jim Brown photo.

Fritz's main lead dog in 1983 was Juneau, one of Joe Sr.'s dogs. Rex and Dakota were also leaders. In 1985 she purchased a special lead dog, Tang, of whom she is very proud. Tang belonged to Joe Redington Sr. and is quite famous. Tang's portrait, along with Joe Redington Sr's, grace the 1984 Gaines Dog Food calendar and the 1985 Tang calendar. Tang is a six-year-old dog in his prime, and has led teams to Nome. In 1985 he was lead dog for Kazuo Kojima, the first Japanese musher to compete in the Iditarod race. She also has one of Tang's sons, Pioneer, whom she feels is of the same quality as Tang.

Kirsch credits Joe Redington Sr. with being a big asset in her learning proper animal care techniques and equipment needs. He has been her mentor and teacher.

> "He's just a pretty incredible man.
> "I guess all my knowledge comes from Joe Sr."

Reflecting on her 1983 race, she notes:

> "I really enjoyed the race and I enjoyed all the volunteers. I was really impressed with the people who live on the coast. Their hospitality was just incredibly fantastic . . . . It's beautiful out there. There's some nasty spots there . . . . I had extremely nice weather. Maybe that's why I'm willing to gamble again.
> "In 1983 it was cold but the weather

was just fantastic. Just as clear as a bell.

"I think I remember all the hard work that was involved. All the hours and hours of preparation.

"I remember the beautiful scenery. That was fantastic.

"I think the most heartbreaking thing to me was after I finished a training season up in the bush. I came down here and got sick. And I had the flu . . . I got it right before the race. Things proceeded to get worse. By the time I hit Rohn River I lost my voice completely. I had an extremely high fever. I think Bobby Lee was the Race Marshall. And he came to me and he said, 'You better take it easy out there girl.' Cause I was pushing pretty hard. And then I was really ill all up the Yukon River. And then I started to come out of it. They flew me in medicine at Rohn River; antibiotics which were really helpful."

She traveled real slow at first as she was real ill. She feels the worst part of the race for her was the beginning — "the first 700 miles" — until she became physically well. In spite of her illness she never considered scratching. She feels she had a very smooth trip, and is very pleased with her dogs' performance during the race.

She has memories of the Farewell Burn area, which she describes as a "real difficult part."

"I got lost in the Burn real bad. I think I lost about six to eight hours there. I fell asleep and then the leader took me off the trail. And then things went from bad to worse. I just couldn't find my way out of there. I just walked long distances punching through the snow because I'd gotten off the trail."

Fritz is a positive person and not one to complain about conditions on the trail. When asked for comments about the trail marking she had no complaints. But she could see the potential benefits of a better flagging and marking system.

"It would be an added benefit if they were better able to mark the trail in a lot of locations. The mountain areas — they were real difficult even though they had been flagged. The high winds took them a few days before I came through. It could be a real severe problem if somebody got lost out there."

Mushers and race officials attempt to keep close tabs on the racers to prevent people from getting dangerously lost or badly hurt. Pilots fly over the trail. Checkers inquire about overdue mushers. The competitors themselves usually watch out for each other.

"I think pretty much everybody keeps an eye on everybody else. Usually by the second day there's three packs. The checker will say, 'Have you seen so and so?' And then they'll say, 'Yeah, he's about three hours from coming in.'

"One guy got stuck out on the ice. Everybody sort of dug into their goodie bags and sent him cookies and hot chocolate.

"You become pretty close. You become really in touch with yourself . . . . You find out what your fellow mushers are really made out of. 'Cause when the going gets tough you're going to see you know who breaks and who does well under pressure."

Fritz Kirsch was raised on a dairy farm in South Dakota. It gave her much experience in dealing with animals on a one to one basis. She remembers the farm as lots of work. Her day began about four in the morning, milking cows. "All I did was chores and work and school." She was "real heavy duty" involved in 4-H. Her skills at dairying and proficiency in citizenship won her a trip to Washington, D.C. Her parents died when she was young, and she has been on her own since her late teens. Her sister still farms the family dairy.

Having always dreamed of coming to Alaska she moved here in 1973. She attended Anchorage Community College for two years of general studies, obtaining an AA degree. In 1978 she moved to Wasilla. The University of Alaska hired her to work in the Dairy Research Center. She remained there for seven years until December 1984. In the early 1980s she put her 4-H skills to work supervising all the Alaska State Fair 4-H entrants. She enjoyed it very much, and found it an ideal way of meeting the Matanuska Valley people.

Kirsch has plans to enter the 1986 Iditarod race unless a recent physical problem makes it impossible. She really enjoys both dairying and mushing dogs. Being a practical and realistic person she is well aware that, to be really competitive as a dog musher, she can only work another job part of the year.

Her main goal in racing the 1986 Iditarod is to better her 1983 race time of 20 days and a few hours. Keeping her dogs year around is a big expense. Recently she figured that it cost her almost $10,000 per year to maintain ten adult dogs, including food and vet bills. That figure does not include any equipment and any race preparation. She feels pretty fortunate so far to have three major sponsors firmed up by October 1985.

One of her major hobbies is arm wrestling. She is quite proficient at it, having qualified for the world championship contest in Petaluma, California, in 1984. While there, she finished third in the world. Local Alaskans paid her entry fees and all her expenses after she qualified on the Alaskan level. She is understandably pleased with her prowess, noting "only one girl has been able to beat me up here." Before going to Petaluma she competed on the Alaska circuit. Hers has been a successful arm wrestling career. She entered her first contest about six years ago and recalls placing third. By the next year, if her memory serves her correctly, she placed first.

A recent venture on her part has been an entrance into the world of candy products. She and a friend were responsible for designing Iditarod candy.

A number of people have run the Iditarod to test themselves. Fritz Kirsch looks at it somewhat differently. Her philosophy is that people test themselves every day. And the Iditarod race is "just spicier" as a test. She has had many tests over the years and has developed a self sufficient style. And her style well fits the dog mushing community and the solitude one finds along the nearly 1,200-mile trek to Nome.

PAM FLOWERS

Excited by accounts of Naomi Uemura's dog sled trek to the North Pole, Pam Flowers changed the course of her life. His exploit led her to dream dreams — big dreams. Why not become the first woman to take a dog team to the South Pole or the North Pole? The petite respiratory therapist set herself on a course which she has doggedly pursued.

When Pam Flowers mushed out of the starting chute of the 1983 Iditarod race, the completion of the Iditarod was not a goal in itself only. It was part of a well developed plan of training for her ultimate goal of a dog sled trip to the North Pole.

She traveled the Iditarod Trail primarily for the experience. She placed 51st in the overall standings of the 54 mushers who made it officially to Nome. Reflecting on the race she feels her most memorable experience was traveling with Norman Vaughan, the 80-year-old musher who has run a number of times. A veteran of Admiral Byrd's 1928 Antarctic Expedition, Vaughn is a legend among dog mushers. Flowers was impressed by his sportsmanship, and found him a lot of fun. She reports deliberately hanging back to travel with him.

"I guess my development in dog mushing has come sort of backwards. A lot of people have become mushers and then formulated some big goal. I did it the other way. I formulated this big goal and then set about acquiring the skills needed to carry out my objective."

She traveled with six or eight mushers and everyone helped each other.

"If you come to a ten-foot bank you have to get up, everyone stops and helps each other up, and then we take off together.

"The funniest thing happened when we were going across the burn. It was night and the trail was hard to see. The temperature was 30 degrees below zero with a strong headwind. I was starting to get really cold when I came to a place where the trail seemed to divide equally to the left and to the right. In the dark I couldn't tell which way to go.

"So I just pulled up into the middle of

Pam Flowers. Photo by Joe Wagener, courtesy of Pam Flowers.

this fork about 100 feet away from the trail, pulled my dogs around in a semicircle and gave everybody a snack. Then I ate a bunch of logan bread . . . about 400 calories per slice, laid down in my sleeping bag and went to sleep.

"I figured I would wait for somebody to go by and see which way they went. While I was laying there four teams went thundering by. Two went to the left and two went to the right. And so I thought, 'Well, what am I supposed to do?' So anyway it seemed so funny because they were all so sure they had gone the right way.

"Pretty soon this guy came back from the left. He said, 'Are you OK there?' And he said, 'This is definitely the right path.' Well, that was the wrong way. Those people ended up going down this little draw and spending the night.

"I decided to stay there a little bit longer and rest. Then Saul Paniptchuk came along and his team wanted to go to the right so we just decided to follow his leader's instinct. That turned out to be the right trail. Then we went off to where we went into the woods. And that's where I met up with Norman Vaughan."

There are many experiences that Flowers remembers. One was during the first hour of the race when she smashed her hand. "It doesn't work correctly yet."

Pam was working as a respiratory therapist at Providence Hospital at the time she ran the Iditarod. Other employees at Providence sponsored about half of her race expenses. She now spends part of her time working as a relief respiratory therapist at Valley Hospital in Palmer. She commutes from her small cabin in the Willow area which she built herself. It is now home to her and 19 dogs. Her male dogs are named after polar explorers such as Robert Scott and Roald Amundsen. Female dogs bear the names of famous women's rights activists.

The 1984 and 1985 spring mushing seasons have been spent mushing dogs along the Alaskan northern beaches and between places like Kotzebue and Barrow and Prudhoe Bay to points eastward. She has been researching and experiencing living in conditions along the northern sea ice as preparation for her planned 1987 expedition to the North Pole with two or three other women. If they are successful they will be the first women to go by a surface means of travel to reach the North Pole (unless a woman does so in 1986).

Physically Pam Flowers is a small person of slender build. Once she decided on her goal of mushing to the Pole she set out to learn to drive dogs. The winter of 1980-81 was spent in Washington State learning about dog mushing. At a Siberian husky group meeting in Virginia she met Bob Crane who told her about Earl and Natalie Norris of the Howling Dog Farm in Willow, Alaska. She spent a year with them, and credits Natalie Norris' patience with enabling her to reach a proficient level.

While living there and helping care for their dogs she chatted with Natalie Norris about her hopes and dreams. Out of this came an agreement with the Norrises to lease land they owned nearby. On this she built the cabin she now calls home. This unpretentious structure is very cozy with pine paneling inside and a storage loft upstairs. She lives simply with none of the modern conveniences urbanites take for granted. A two-burner Coleman stove for cooking, a woodstove for heat, and a small area on which to lay her sleeping bag add to its rustic simplicity. In an area with considerable subzero temperatures she uses about two cords of firewood a year. In the winter she hikes a mile to the main road. Since she has no telephone she has a message post for phone messages received by a neighbor. There is no indoor plumbing.

Living alone with her dogs, the solitude now accepted as part of her life has roots in her childhood. Both parents worked, and she lived in an area without children for playmates. She developed ways of entertaining herself. One is reading. She reads extensively, "only nonfiction." Her built-in bookshelves are packed with books of polar and northern adventures. Another 500 plus books are stored outside.

She has a slide show she presents in New York, Chicago, Washington, D.C. and elsewhere as she looks for financial backing for her 1987 polar trek. Having carried the required Iditarod Committee mail in the Iditarod race, she had a number of the ones she carried signed by mushers in Nome. For her 1987 North Pole expedition she is also planning to carry mail to raise money to defray the expedition's costs. Costs for her American Women's North Pole Expedition are estimated at a couple hundred thousand dollars. The major cost is transportation.

While some mushers run the Iditarod to test themselves, others run for the competition. Others run for the experience. No matter what the reason, most find the people they meet along the way some of the most memorable and enjoyable parts of their experience. Pam Flowers was no different.

She can definitely say the Iditarod was her first long dog team trip along the journey of life. And a prelude to her ultimate dream of leading the first successful women's dog team expedition to the North Pole. A dream fueled by a Japanese adventurer whom Flowers credits as having more influence on her life than any other person. Ironically, Uemura lost his life in Alaska after becoming the first person to make a solo winter ascent of Mt. McKinley.

In 1983 Jon Van Zyle's Iditarod poster was entitled "Alone on the Crest of your Dreams." Pam Flowers ran the Iditarod that year. That theme is certainly her theme as she continues her progress toward another test on the polar icecap.

BEVERLY JERUE MASEK

Beverly Jerue Masek as a 19-year-old entered the Iditarod race in 1983. Raised in the village of Anvik, she grew up along the Iditarod Trail. Entering as Stuckagain Heights Team No. 2, she trained in the Anchorage area with Jan Masek. Beverly became acquainted with the Iditarod race by helping mushers Rudy Demoski and Ken Chase from Anvik in their training for the Iditarod for several years.

Although both Beverly Jerue and Jan Masek ended up scratching from the race at McGrath, Beverly remembers her experience as one in which she had no problems with her dogs. However, it was a very different situation than she had expected. She had trained well with many camping experiences. Utilizing the trails around Stuckagain Heights and the Tudor Sled Dog Track in Anchorage, she had lots of experience with uphill terrain. She also had lots of experience with moose. Yet during her time in the race she saw virtually no wildlife. Only once was the stillness of the wilderness broken by sounds of the wild. Near Rohn River and Farewell Lake she heard wolves howling while camping.

One of the new experiences the Iditarod gave her was the long hours and no showers. "You're going all the time. You can't go home and relax" at the end of a long day.

Her decision to scratch came because of an unfortunate experience on the trail. While descending Rainy Pass she and Jan Masek came to a place with a narrow ravine. There were four spruce poles across it. It was very icy. She was unable to stop. Another musher was camped out, blocking the trail. She fell into the gully. Still the musher refused to vacate the trail. Both she and Jan Masek filed a protest about the incident. No one from the race committee seemed to do anything about it. In

Beverly Jerue Masek. Photo courtesy of B.J. Masek.

spite of that regretful occurrence she remembers Rainy Pass pleasantly. Traveling through during daylight hours she was able to "see everything."

The daughter of Carl and Marie Jerue, she grew up in the village of Anvik, Alaska. Her mother used to race in the dog races there at the time of village get togethers. The family lived a lifestyle in harmony with the traditional way of life. Although both parents worked seasonal jobs the family trapped in the winter and fished summers. Her father worked summers on construction and road projects. Her mother works summers in the clinic as a health aide and the rest of the year as a teacher's aide in school. She is the sixth of eight children.

Beverly Jerue Masek came to Anchorage in 1981. At the time of the 1983 Iditarod she was employed as the dining room manager at Stuckagain Heights. Her husband, Jan Masek, was a partner in the business. She had first met him in 1979 when he was in Anvik buying fish there. On March 5, 1984, the two were married at the Finger Lake checkpoint during the Iditarod Trail Race. The wedding took place in the beautiful outdoor surroundings in front of musher Gene Leonard's cabin. It was presided over by Norman Vaughan, a veteran Iditarod racer, and Jeff Parker. Gene and June Leonard were best man and matron of honor. After the wedding her bridegroom continued in the race.

In April 1985, the Maseks moved to the Chena Hot Springs Lodge northeast of Fairbanks. There they are managing the Lodge which is the location for one of the checkpoints on the Yukon Quest International Sled Dog Race, the 1,000-plus mile race held between Fairbanks, Alaska and Whitehorse, Yukon Territory, Canada.

In September 1985, Beverly became a mother. Little Michael Jan Albert Masek has slowed her down a little. She still plans to mush dogs and hopes to race in the Bull's Eye-Angel Creek 125 race. She likes the quietness of the Chena Hot Springs area, and finds it a good place for running dogs.

Beverly Masek is a woman of her convictions. She is also willing to stand up and spend her own money to defend them. In early 1984 she sued the Bureau of Land Management over the Iron Dog Snowmobile Race. She won the suit. Seven violations were found. The suit was over the issue of the race proceeding through Native lands without first obtaining permission from the owners of the lands. The court decision found that the Bureau of Land Management only had jurisdiction over about 140 miles of the Iditarod National Historic Trail. The bylaws of the National Historic Trail state that permission be obtained from the owners and Native corporations. That permission had not been obtained. Beverly spent about $7,000 of her own money in that endeavor.

An event she recalls is the trip to Washington, D.C., she and her husband, along with Gene and June Leonard and Edna and Emmitt Peters, made for President Ronald Reagan's inauguration in January 1985. The three couples planned to drive their three dog teams and sleds in the Inaugural Parade. Extremely cold weather forced the cancellation of the parade. However, the previous Saturday afternoon the Alaskan contingent assembled on the front lawn of the Capitol. There they gave rides to Alaskan Senators Ted Stevens and Frank Murkowski. There was press coverage of the event, and Beverly and her husband were filmed by "Good Morning America" crews as mushers from Alaska. The film was shown on television on Inauguration Day.

1985 Iditarod Champion Libby Riddles with lead dogs Axle and Dugan at Nome finish line. ©*1985 Jeff Schultz.*

CHAPTER 6

New Women Entrants: 1984-1985

Nine women were among the 67 racers starting on the trail in 1984. One of the four rookie women entrants was Kari Skogen of Norway, the first woman from a foreign nation to enter the race. The next year two women from France, Claire Philip and Monique Bene, ran the race.

Susan Butcher again placed second in the 1984 race (see Chapter 4). By now one of the best known Iditarod mushers, she was one of the favorites to win in 1985. However, the first night in the 1985 race her team was attacked by a moose. Two of her dogs were killed and several others seriously injured. She dropped out of the race. In spite of Butcher's race tragedy, 1985 did provide the hoped for Iditarod race victory by a woman.

"Libby Wins!" became the headline on March 20, 1985. Libby Riddles (see Chapter 4), who finished in the money the two other times she raced, surprised most observers when she took the lead at Unalakleet and never relinquished it. Her dramatic drive into a blinding storm on the ice from Shaktoolik captured the hearts of many, and surprised top mushers not far behind her. Her unexpected victory boosted interest in the race, and gave the race much national and international media coverage.

DIANA DRONENBURG

When Diana Dronenburg and her husband Ray Dronenburg ran the 1984 Iditarod, it was actually their second race as a team, but was the first time in Iditarod history that a husband and wife ran together in competition with each other in the Iditarod. Ray had finished 40th in 1983. Both hoped to better that mark in 1984. Unfortunately it was not to be for Ray as an unexplained illness in his dogs forced him to scratch from the race in Galena, nearly 700 miles from the race start. In spite of this, Diana notes they still have the honor of being the first husband and wife Iditarod mushers to sign the "immortalized" ceiling at Cripple checkpoint. (Note: Mushers passing the checkpoint since 1978 have signed their names to the ceiling.)

Pressing on from Galena, Diana entered Nome in 27th position — respectable for a rookie musher. Reflecting on the experience she notes:

"We left Rainy Pass Lodge around 5 P.M. heading for the pass itself and the next checkpoint, Rohn Roadhouse. I had heard many horror stories about the pass and was slightly nervous about this part of the trail. The dogs, after just coming off a 24-hour rest, were in a

Diana Dronenburg and one of her dogs. N. Nielsen photo.

fantastic mood and wanted to run and run fast. I kept turning around to Ray and saying, 'Is this part considered the pass?' and he'd say, 'No, keep going,' and I kept on. I, of course, was interested in knowing when were about to hit the bad part. Then possibly I could brace myself.

"The dogs at one point stopped, and I could not coax them into going again. It was pretty dark so I went ahead to take a look. They were definitely smarter than me. What lay ahead was a cliff. Had the dogs continued to go ahead we (the dogs and I) could have been seriously injured. I had praise for Dolly and Amber at that point! We continued and, with a few short stops for snacking, the dogs made Rohn Roadhouse in just under five hours. The rest of the way was just fun running. It was, generally speaking, an enjoyable night with the dogs."

Each musher has many stories about their dogs. Diana is no exception. One of her favorite dogs was her former lead dog Sally. Sally went to Nome on Steve Rieger's team in 1983 and on Diana's team in 1984. Sally was purchased for a nominal price from a well-known sprint musher because her attitude towards running made her appear less than an ideal racing dog. In fact she had been named Stupid. She had never been considered for lead.

"Why would you consider a dog that didn't like to work and had the name of Stupid? There was something that I liked about her so I took her.

"One day while training I got into some deep snow .... I told this new lead dog, 'Lobo, Gee.' He gave me a look as if to say, 'Naw, you're not serious.' I said, 'Lobo, Gee.' So he did. He jumped into this pretty deep snow .... Now Sally was just along for the ride. She had not worked a bit. Then all of a sudden she perked up and just lunged into her harness. I thought, 'She is stupid. She actually likes the deep snow!' I put her up in lead with Lobo and she loved it. From there on out, she worked well and was a very vital part of my team."

Unfortunately Sally died the following fall. Sally had just one litter of pups. They were born the summer of 1984, just a few months before death. Diana has hopes they will prove to be good dogs.

The best lead dogs on the Dronen-burg lot now are Dolly, Shadow and Ruby. Dolly, at 35 pounds, is the favorite due to her personality and "just plain gutsy attitude." Dolly spent a great deal of time in the 1985 race leading bigger, stronger, but less smart lead dogs out of real serious spots. "Ray talks of winds strong enough to move the sled sideways like a pendulum on a clock and Dolly just pulling forward." Dolly was also on Diana's 1984 team. Diana recalls her really coming into her own during that race.

"When all else failed Dolly would come to the rescue: water, glare ice, no snow at all; it didnt' matter. She went through it all and still kept her great attitude."

In relating her own race experience Diana talks about acquiring sun poisoning.

"One day my cheeks began to get these small red bumps that were extremely itchy. My face then began to swell, and pretty soon I looked like a chipmunk. While on the race I didn't know what it was or how to treat it. So I did nothing and the swelling continued. By the time I hit the finish line in Nome it looked like I had an extra 50 pounds on me. But that didn't matter. What was far more important was seeing the lights of Nome and having all these people cheering me on until I finally made it. After being on the trail for 15 days I reached Nome. Even finishing in 27th position and, being out of the money, I still was a winner."

Diana is one of three children. She was born and raised in California. Her sister lives in Fairbanks and her brother in California. She had step sisters and brothers while growing up and considers them all part of her family. Her hobbies include all types of sports and playing the guitar. The music is for her own enjoyment, but whenever she is angry or frustrated, playing the guitar seems to calm her.

Getting a team ready for an Iditarod takes a great deal of time, energy and a lot of money. Diana has the time and a great deal of energy. Ray has the opportunity to provide the money. Together they work as a team.

Diana enjoys both sprint and long distance racing. She has come to realize that you cannot do both well in the same year. The 1985-86 racing season she will concentrate on sprints and Ray will run the Iditarod. 1987 she hopes to run the Iditarod.

Both Ray and Diana plan to keep the Iditarod part of their life, but with the rising costs and the amount of time spent on training they will only enter one Iditarod team a year. When Diana next races the Iditarod she hopes to stay further away from home while training the dogs. She feels the dogs and the mushers became too "kennel happy" last year during training, and it may have affected the team.

The Dronenburgs live in the Willow Pass area with an inspiring view of Willow Creek out their dining room. Their four-year-old son, John, keeps her active. In addition to her family responsibilities, her life is now focused on running the kennel, raising, training and racing the dogs.

Diana works in Barrow, Alaska, during the spring and summer months. She originally moved to Alaska to make money to return to college studies in the field of law. She never left Alaska. While she would like to continue her college education, Diana Dronenburg seems to have found her niche at present amidst the 70 or so dogs at the D&D Kennels and the beautiful Alaskan countryside.

KARI SKOGEN

Kari Skogen, at age 21, became the first woman musher from another country to race the Iditarod. She placed 35th in the 1984 race.

"When I was in high school I heard about Mari Hoe, a Norwegian girl that had been over in the States to run dogs. I wrote to Mari and asked her if she knew somebody that I could go to and learn about dog mushing, Nome style. Mari gave me the address of the Norrises with whom she had stayed."

In December 1982, Kari arrived in Willow to begin training. She spent five months there and states, "Earl and Natalie learned me everything

Kari Skogen. Jim Brown photo.

about training dogs."

Her first winter in Willow she met a Californian who encouraged her to go for her dreams. That Siberian husky fan told her that if she would take a team of purebred Siberian huskies in the race, she would help sponsor her. So she came back the following year to train for the Iditarod. That friendship, kindled by love for the talented Siberian husky, remains part of her strategy for obtaining sponsors for the 1986 Iditarod.

Kari, the youngest of three children, grew up in the mountains of southern Norway not far from Norway's tallest mountain. She lives in farm country, surrounded by a large extended family. Its climate is similar to Willow, Alaska. Considered the driest part of Norway, it is nestled east of high mountains. Its snowfalls are not very deep but stay late, providing skiing in May in the mountains. She enjoys skiing in the mountains with friends. Some of her friends had dogs they would take "skijouring" (harnessed with a rope tied around their waists so the dogs pulled them).

Kari did not race competitively until 1981 in Norway. Then she entered a one-dog class race with a German shepherd and won. She ran again in 1982. In the one-, two- and three-dog classes, racers go behind their dogs on skis, not on foot. In the five-dog and up categories, they mush "Nome style." The race in her area is a 50-mile camping race. The first day you go 30 miles and camp out that night. The next day the last 20 miles is done.

Kari remembers having a lot of wet, rainy weather in the 1984 Iditarod. She enjoyed the race. She traveled by herself most of the time, but constantly passed or was passed by Fran Bennis, Calvin Lauwer and Armen Khatchikian (a rookie from Italy). Her main lead dogs were Chenan, Karu and Short.

She was only seriously lost once in the race. Testimony to her acumen is that it happened when she was less than 80 miles from Nome.

"After I left White Mountain the last night, I lost the trail up there in the mountains.... I fooled around for three or four hours before I found the trail... back where I'd been before. Then I didn't do the same mistake. I looked around a little more carefully. With the dogs you know sometime you rely on the dogs because you think they know where to go. You may let them decide when you don't have any idea. A lot of other people had taken the same trail so that's what they did."

Another kind of difficult experience was when the dogs didn't want to eat.

"I tried to do everything. You'd feed them by hand, different kinds of stuff. Like I had to make patties and divide them in two, in four, in six. Try everything to make them eat.... And you have to get water into them. And that makes you nervous because they get dehydrated. That was the most frustrating I think."

There were many nice experiences in the race. Perhaps tops on Kari's list of these are her experiences with the natives along the trail. She was invited to their homes, offered meals, and was able to get a few hours sleep in their homes. It was a nice switch from "frozen sandwiches."

Kari hopes to place better in the 1986 Iditarod. She plans "to get better training" on the dogs by taking them on more overnight camping trips to get them more used to eating on the trail. She hopes for less rain and water to go through, but will be prepared if it's there. In 1984 she carried 800 dog booties. She was sewing booties on rainy September 1985 days.

Kari sewed much of her clothing for the 1984 Iditarod, including a Gortex parka. She made her reindeer fur hat from reindeer she and her father had hunted in Norway, lining it with wool. Hand knitted wool socks add warmth to her gear. Her mother has knitted many pairs of socks for the 1986 race. She estimates her cost for running the 1984 race was about $8,000 thanks to Earl and Natalie Norris.

"I can make some of the gear better than I can buy in the store." In fact, money can't buy some of what she has, such as handmade overpants. She did not suffer from foot blisters thanks to wearing a pair of Norwegian felt shoes at appropriate times when bunny boots weren't needed.

Kari feels that dog sleds and the Iditarod race provide an excellent way to see the countryside. In talking with Kari her spirit of adventure comes through. She combines the quiet warmth of a friendly young lady who is pursuing her dreams.

After a year of furniture making school in Norway, she returned to the Norris household in August 1985. She had crafted designer chairs, a bed, cabinets and other beautiful furniture which now grace her parents' home in Norway. This craftsperson plans to return home to Norway in the spring of 1986 for more education.

On March 1, 1986, Kari will take her place with many Nome-bound mushers. With 14 to 16 dogs she will again mush into the wilderness. No matter what the outcome she will give the race her best, and add a store of memories to her already thrill-packed past.

FRANCINE BENNIS

Francine Bennis, a native of Niagara Falls, New York, entered her first Iditarod race in 1984. She placed 38th. A graduate of the University of

Francine Bennis and lead dog Amethyst. R. Nielsen photo.

Alaska at Fairbanks, with a B.S. in biology/geology, she first visited Alaska in 1975. The stimulation of the north country made her know that she wanted to run dogs.

In 1978, she began running a four-dog team that belonged to a friend who had left Alaska for the winter. The winter of 1978-1979, she and three other friends began planning a dog team trip from Hudson's Bay to Great Slave Lake, and then by canoe along some rivers in northern Canada. They headed to Bristol Bay for the summer. They had purchased a dog team. When trip plans fell through, three of them divided the team. In 1980 when she was in Dillingham, she met up with Joe Redington Sr. and Dick Mackay. The talk turned to the Iditarod. The idea of running the Iditarod became tangible at that time.

Reflecting on her race experience, she recalls, "It was great! I had such a good time." She felt the race was "a piece of cake compared to the training." She had so many financial restrictions during training that she knew by December 1983 she could not be competitive in the race. Coming from a family where her mother was very practical, she had to convince herself that running the race was something more than frivolous when it was costing her so much money. In September she had decided it was a worthwhile venture to experience. By the end of March, and the 1984 Iditarod, she was sure of it.

After running the race she sees what it can be. She feels the Iditarod race is important to Alaska. If for one fleeting moment there is a "brief shining of the human spirit," then it is worth it. The spectacular countryside and the spirit of cooperation impressed her. She met so many kind people she was overwhelmed. She feels she couldn't have made it to Nome without the help she had from many friends. "So many people did so much for me." In addition to her friends there were all those people along the trail, strangers, who were so warm and so giving. She feels there are not too many experiences of that kind in the world. She hopes that the race will always retain that kind of feeling.

Of her memories with her dogs, the most profound is of making it into Nome. When the dogs left Safety they were so excited, they seemed to know they were almost there. Waterloo, her leader, was jumping three feet in the air. "Somehow she knew," even though she had never been to Nome. As she arrived in Nome her dogs were trotting along Front Street. A little child suddenly jumped in the middle of the street. The dogs just stopped. While the child was getting yelled at by his mother, Bennis was trying to get her dog team started again. She had to go in front of her team and pull her leader to get the team going.

She was impressed by the dogs' tenacity. It was awesome to realize their capacities. Her leader, Amethyst, was one of two dogs she originally purchased from Joe Redington Sr. at the end of the 1982 fishing season. She is a "real morale booster" who went as far as Safety. In addition to her own dogs, she leased a number from Joe Redington Sr. Leased leaders included Sitka and Waterloo. She feels each dog did something outstanding along the way, although none of the dogs did so consistently throughout the race.

She feels that once you've raced the Iditarod, "it gets in your blood." She plans to run it again in a couple of years. When she does run again, she will be running to win. She feels that it is hard to justify the expense just for fun. It's a "costly venture." It's a year around proposition.

One of Bennis's recurring thoughts was:

"I felt I could tip my hat to Joe Redington Sr. for pursuing the idea of the Iditarod race, and his persistence in following it through to its fruition. It is something that has become so inspirational to so many people. I think it is great!"

Bennis is a commercial fisherman in the Bristol Bay fishery. One of the problems with fishing there is that she can't keep her dogs in the bay in the summertime. She also works as a union laborer.

She is the youngest of four daughters in her family. Her father, who will be 81 in January 1986, has been very supportive of her Alaskan lifestyle and her dog team and Iditarod experience. As a young man he tried twice to get the Army to assign him to Alaska but was unsuccessful. Her mother was initially skeptical of her daughter's plans, especially of her spending at least $10,000 to "freeze" herself. Later comments to others indicate her mother warmed up to the idea, in spite of her practical outlook.

Bennis's current goals are focused on her desire to obtain a Bristol Bay fishing permit. She has recently been spending most of her energies on that goal. She owns a house in the former copper mining community of Kennecott, Alaska, which eventually she plans to fix up and possibly make into a small lodge. She would like to run dog trips out of there. She is thinking about perhaps returning for further college studies in the fisheries area.

Her "heart is in the Iditarod" and she hopes to be on the race trail in a couple of years. She really loves the countryside it passes through. She is a skier and the mountains hold a special lure for her. But first she needs to get her fishing plans secured. Then she wants to obtain good sponsors to put together a competitive team. A cheery, enthusiastic person she will no doubt persevere in her plans and dreams, and will again take the opportunity to enter and race the challenge of the Iditarod Trail.

MIKI COLLINS

Miki Collins, a 24-year-old from Lake Minchumina, Alaska, had mushed dogs for 10 years before she entered the 1984 Iditarod.

> "When I sat with him in the snow he gazed at me with his steady golden-brown eyes and I knew he'd pull until he dropped. He was Loki's son, and a dog with more raging determination than Loki was never born. Streak had some of that strength but I saw in his eyes that he trusted me not to ask him to do something he couldn't.
>
> "I reached down and hugged him tightly, and then quietly went inside. I signed the check-in sheet. 'Scratched,' I wrote."[1]

So ended Miki's seven-year dream

Miki Collins at start of 1984 Iditarod. Photo by Frances Mitchell, McGrath, courtesy of M. Collins.

of running the Iditarod. In spite of the decision to scratch there were both good as well as bad experiences associated with the Iditarod.

> "After training in January and February in temperatures ranging from zero to 40 below, the 30 to 45 degree weather we'd been having since leaving Anchorage on March 3 devastated my big, heavy-coated dogs, slowing them until we were at the trail end of the 67 mushers in the race. Still, the scenery thrilled me as we traveled up the narrow ravine, mountains towering hundreds of feet above us on either side of the trail. Only the bright beams of headlights shone where other mushers were.
>
> "Daylight found us twisting back down Dalzel Canyon, zig-zagging back and forth across the tiny creek, crashing down ten-foot banks and dodging open holes where ice had collapsed into the water."[2]

Taking her 24-hour mandatory layover at Rohn, Miki inventoried the toll on her team. Comet could go no further. Another dog had a wrenched shoulder.

> "Most mushers were running 12 to 16 dogs picked from kennels of 20 to 60. But I had left with every dog I own and had more 'lemons' in my team than I cared to admit."[2]

Taking turns breaking trail with Bob Sunder and Dave Aisenbrey, the three fell more than a full day behind the other mushers.

> "Past midnight we reached the little native village of Nikolai on the Kuskokwim River. Holy Moses, I felt good to be back in Kusko country. After having carried the lame dog for 20 miles, I gave up and left him there, going on to McGrath very early the following morning with nine dogs.
>
> "I knew the team was in bad shape; two to three dogs were dragging as much as pulling, but I wasn't sure I could afford to drop them."[3]

After a luxurious 15-hour respite in McGrath, Miki departed. At Takotna she was treated to coconut pie and lemonade. At Ophir the welcome hot food was interspersed with lots of dog talk and advice from "Robby" Roberts.

> "We moved on into the blackness, paralleling the Innoko River. I had a dog in season and several of the males were fighting. Three dogs started dragging . . .
>
> "The remainder of that night and the following day into Cripple had been horrible. At times I was walking in front of the dogs, coaxing them along. Of the nine dogs, one was in the sled and three were still dragging. Sparky, although pulling gamely, developed dehydration . . . . Streak, my other big wheel dog, had bad feet . . . . Only three dogs were in good health."[1]

Then came the painful decision. To scratch, or to risk hurting her team more, only to scratch later. Miki decided to scratch. One year later, in March 1985, her twin sister Julie was able to use some of Miki's team to run in the over 1,000 mile Yukon Quest Race between Whitehorse, Yukon Territory, and Fairbanks, Alaska. Julie finished 20th of 34 teams.

Collins grew up at Lake Minchumina with her twin sister and her brother. Her mother taught the children with state correspondence courses through the seventh grade. For the next nine years the children stayed in Fairbanks, going to high school and college. She and Julie took off a semester during college to trap in their home area. All three children earned B.S. degrees in biology at the University of Alaska, Fairbanks. Her father was an administrator with the F.A.A. Her mother is a geologist.

When she was 14 she and her

brother began putting together a team to use on a trapline. Her brother only used it one winter, and then the twins took it over gradually until all the dogs now belong to them.

After college she and Julie returned home. They now pursue a subsistence bush type lifestyle. They hunt moose, fish, and freeze fish for their dogs. They trap each year for several months, beginning in November. Summer is spent fishing for the dogs, gardening, picking "gallons and gallons of berries" (strawberries, raspberries, blueberries and cranberries) and making handicrafts. She and her sister provide the moose meat and garden for the family; her parents "supply the evaporated milk, pilot bread and peanut butter."

They live in the large family log home with solar panels while their parents are at the lake. When their parents are gone they live winters in a smaller cabin which is easier to heat. Their home is located on land that was originally a fur farm.

Miki and her sister use dogs because they prefer them to snow machines. They also have too large a trapline (70 miles) to cover on foot. They use dogs to haul freight across the lake. They have dogs because they prefer them, not because dogs are less expensive. Collins feels they spend as much or more on their dogs as most trappers spend on snowmachines.

Their trapline was trapped for many years, beginning about 1920, by Slim Carlson, until a few years before his death at 89 in 1975. Miki feels he probably influenced her attitude and aspirations as much as any one person.

Miki Collins has never been particularly interested in dog racing. The Iditarod is "something I wanted to do . . . maybe just because if you want to find out how good (or bad) your dogs are you have to prove them against others." She wants to run it again because she knows she can do it, and wants to have done it.

Collins, a free lance writer, has had articles published in *Alaska Magazine* and a number of other publications. Her graphic account of her Iditarod experiences (quoted from earlier) appeared in the Alaska Airlines flight magazine in March 1985. She hand spins her dogs' hair into delightful functional hats, mittens, and a variety of other articles. She also makes items from fur she traps along her trapline. Her 65- to 75-pound trapline dogs average 15 to 20 pounds heavier than today's average Iditarod race dog. She also mushes her team on long winter treks, traveling as much as 600 miles on these adventures.

This hardy bush Alaskan maintains a dog team for many of the same reasons pioneer Alaskans used teams along the Iditarod Trail early in the 20th century. She loves running and working her dogs. Racing is not her main goal. Living her independent lifestyle, "to get everything out of life I possibly can and be as happy as I can," is. She is concerned that competition for the land, new roads, and other pressures will cause her way of life to be lost.

BETSY McGUIRE

Betsy McGuire of Takotna, Alaska, became a last-minute entrant in the 1985 Iditarod race when her partner, Frank Torres, broke his leg eight days before the race. Making the decision to run his team the Tuesday before the Saturday race start, she was still purchasing gear when the first mushers left the starting chute on Fourth Avenue. In spite of her last-minute entry, she finished in 29th position, the second highest place for women entered in the race.

> "In some ways it might have been easier for me because I was so ignorant of so many things . . . . I didn't have any idea of what was coming. I just plowed right into it."

McGuire came to Alaska the summer of 1978 as a Camp Fire Girls' swimming instructor in the villages of McGrath, Nikolai, Takotna and Holy Cross. She met Torres who was

Betsy McGuire. R. Nielsen photo.

also a swimming instructor. In Nikolai she acquired a puppy, Nikolai, one of her race leaders; and Torres acquired AK, a male husky who was also on her Iditarod team.

After the summer, McGuire left Alaska. Torres stayed. When she couldn't keep her dog where she was living, she and Nikolai returned to Takotna where Torres was living. They obtained a couple more dogs and began running them for fun. Then they began to use them to haul wood and for transportation, since they only purchased a snowmobile in late 1985.

The driveway of their cabin just out of Takotna is on the Iditarod Trail. As the race went by each March, Torres' interest in running it increased. The number of their dogs grew. They bred dogs and purchased a few. Their dogs average 50 to 60 pounds, larger than the average Iditarod racing dog. Four of the fifteen dogs she began the race with did not belong to her or Torres. She dropped two of them at Rabbit Lake checkpoint because "it was too much dog power for me."

In 1985, race rules required all rookies to have completed a 200 mile qualifying race. Fortunately for McGuire, she had run the McGrath Mail Trail 200 two weeks before the race. On the other hand, the weather was very cold (−40 degrees), and she and other racers had problems with the sharp ice crystals cutting up the dogs' feet. At night temperatures dropped even more.

Making the decision to run the Iditarod was difficult. Torres and KSKO McGrath radio announcer Will Peterson talked to her about it. Dick Mackey also encouraged her to run. The KSKO station manager (where she was planning to work Peterson's schedule so he could cover the race on the trail) told her, "if there was something she had to do, the radio station was behind her all the way." That took away her last excuse. After she made the decision to run she fed the dogs that evening. They were really fired up. She knew then she had made the right decision.

In the beginning of the race she did not even know some of the dogs who weren't her own. She worried about not knowing how to motivate the dogs once they got tired. It took her a while but she finally got "that repertoire with the dogs."

Another fear she had was for her own survival. It was very cold, perhaps 60 below, on the Yukon. "I was freezing. It was really cold." Eventually she discovered there was always somebody close by, even though she might not see anyone for hours unless she stopped.

Her best runs in the race came in her home area: Nikolai to McGrath and McGrath to Ophir. She was caught in McGrath by the second race freeze as she was getting her team ready to leave. After that the dogs seemed to know McGuire was mushing them — that Torres wasn't going to take over. So the dogs settled down and enjoyed themselves. She thought:

"Of course the dogs are enjoying this . . . . Heavens, they're getting constant attention and good food continually . . . . They were getting the absolute best treatment in the whole world. Of course they're going to love it."

She feels the race is the best time of the dogs' whole year. The only regret she had about the end of the race was:

"The 'repertoire' that a musher gains with his or her team during the race is very special — and that was coming to an end.

"For about two weeks we really had our stuff together. And knew who each other was, and what to expect. And it really changed my attitude on a lot of the dogs in the team. One of the dogs who was (a particular problem to her in the past) . . . . I really thought, 'Wow! He really is a good dog.'"

Her main leader in the race was her original dog, Nikolai. Nikolai is a natural leader and is fast. Her other leaders included AK, Petruska, Sarge (who wasn't her dog), and Derrick. At the beginning of the race she had much to learn, including experimenting in what positions to put the dogs during the race.

Once she started the race she never thought more than a day ahead. She just went. She never thought more than a checkpoint ahead. When she got to Shaktoolik she thought:

"Gee, maybe I'm going to make it all the way . . . . Here I am. It's blowing . . . and I made it through all that."

She credits traveling with Nathan Underwood as helping her find Shaktoolik in the windstorm. He kept saying, "I know we've got to keep following this." It was totally dark the entire time she was out there. She and Nathan took turns leading. She tried to leave villages in the daytime when it was practical. There are so many trails outside of the villages, it is easy to lose the race trail in the dark.

She feels her traveling companions added much to her race experience. In the villages she and the racers who were at the back half of the pack were given just as big a welcome as those in the lead. She feels their welcome never wore out. She was impressed by how good people along the coast were to all the Iditaroders.

McGuire preferred to travel with other racers. Nevertheless, she did spend a few nights alone. Enroute to Elim was one such night. It was really windy. That night she got separated from her companions as her dogs couldn't keep up with them. She couldn't see where she was going. She had trouble finding the markers on the ice. She couldn't find her bearings. She was afraid when she walked away from the dogs, looking for markers, she would not be able to find the team again. So she camped. She lay in her sled, in her sled bag. Then daylight came faster than expected. She could see exactly where she had to go. She was only about 50 feet off the trail, but was pointed away from the trail.

Resuming her trek she passed Moses Point. Then she came upon a weather station. There she was resting when about 10 teams pulled up behind her. Nathan Underwood was among them. No one could figure how she got there first.

Later she sneaked out of White Mountain, getting a big jump on several sleeping mushers. She was resting near the top of Topkok Hill when she heard Nathan Underwood's whistle. In the end he beat her to Nome by 20 minutes.

McGuire remembers getting into Nome as the hottest day of her race. Finding the finish line was more of a problem than she expected. It wasn't well marked. She'd go on to a street and wasn't sure if it was the trail. Her dogs were kind of "people shy." She ended up leading her team down Front Street until Nikolai heard Torres' whistle in the crowd of onlookers. She was thrilled and amazed by the number of folks from the McGrath area who greeted her there since she arrived three days after the leaders.

McGuire, a volunteer disc jockey from McGrath these days, grew up in the city of Madison, Wisconsin. Her father owned a clothing store. Her mother, a housewife, now sells real estate. She and her five siblings were athletic. The family had no animals.

"I had wanted a puppy all my life. Here I was finally on my own. Here were these puppies. And this guy was willing to give me one. So I took it."

And so Nikolai entered her life. Besides her dogs McGuire has a cat, D.J. She finds cats "great," and a different kind of a pet than sled dogs.

She considers Alaska her home. She is excited now as her first child is due around New Year's 1986. She feels real content with her life and lifestyle. She looks forward to the changes and challenges of being a mother. Torres has plans to run the 1986 Iditarod. She wants him to run. The dogs are ready. Yet the training needed for the race will make it difficult for Torres to be in Anchorage for the entire time she needs to be there for the baby's birth.

Betsy McGuire, in the best of Alaskan tradition, stepped in when she was needed. Without much time to really prepare she learned on the trail and had a good time with her dogs. She is truly an Alaskan!

CLAIRE PHILIP

Claire Philip and her husband Jacques of By-Thomery, France, became the first couple to both complete the Iditarod race together in the same year. They entered in 1985, and were the first couple from a foreign nation to enter. Jacques finished in 21st position and Claire in 37th position of the 61 entrants.

The Philips' interest in dog mushing was sparked by seeing some photographs of the Iditarod and Fur Rendezvous races at a camp in the Alps. Four years before entering the Iditarod they traveled to Alaska to learn more about the sport. They spent about six months with Earl and Natalie Norris at The Howling Dog Farm in Willow before traveling to the Yukon Territory. There they spent a few months in a small cabin before returning to France. They took several sled dogs home with them.

Back in France, the Philips decided to travel to Norway to purchase more dogs to build a dog team. They became "hooked" on sled dogs. Her husband began entering dog races. He raced first in the five-dog class, and then the seven-dog class.

They began searching for sponsors to finance their dream of running the Iditarod. The search was less successful than they hoped, but still managed to provide them with the support that made it possible to enter. Air France provided transportation for them and their dogs. Barres Freres made four sleds for them, and Elan Sport gave them special cold weather clothing. Parlez-Vous-Francais Bakery of Anchorage made them special nutritional bread for the race.

Claire came to Alaska in September 1984 to help her husband with his race training and preparations (he arrived in August). The Philips brought over seven of their own dogs from France. Joe Redington Sr. helped them with their training. They leased the additional dogs needed from him. He gave them an old truck to fix up for transportation.

> "The engine was hanging in a tree. The radiator was in the woods, and all the bolts were everywhere. Then we had to put a dog box on it."[4]

He let them build a shelter to live in during their stay at his Trapper Creek training camp.

When Claire Philip journeyed to Alaska she had no plans to enter the race. She saw herself as helping her husband and entering one of the local races. She ran Don's Iditarod 200, finishing in 21st position. This race qualified her to run the Iditarod. Joe Redington Sr. had some extra dogs that she could use, so she made the decision to try the long run to Nome also.

Claire did not see herself as being really competitive. Her goal was to finish the race and do as well as she could. Her husband summed it up:

> "She doesn't have much of a chance to be very competitive. She's always taking care of the dogs. Besides, I usually always take the best dogs."[4]

Looking back on the race Claire feels happy she ran. She feels although it is hard to run the Iditarod, that anyone can do it if they take their time and take good care of their dogs. She feels she did as well as she could. She would like to run the race again and do even better. So does her husband. Both feel running again depends on their having good sponsors.

During the race at times Claire had her doubts. She agonized about whether her decision to run would cost her husband some race positions, as some of her dogs might have been an added asset to his team. Yet most of the time she smiled. Donna Gentry, race marshall, remembers seeing her really enjoy what she was doing. She really loved her dogs.

At their home in a small French village, their love of their dogs impresses visitors. When Susan Carroll, newspaper reporter for *The Frontiersman*, visited them last summer she noticed the differences between the way their dogs lived and Alaskan kennels often appear. Both the Philips and Monique Bene had their dogs in a fenced-in kennel. The Philips treated their dogs like children. Their dog lot was very clean and spotless. There were always at least three dogs in the large country farmhouse. The farmhouse, which belongs to Claire's parents, has a garden, fruit trees and a garden pond on its couple acres. The dogs often run free and enjoy the garden pond.

Claire Philip notes that their dogs are "pure breed Siberian husky dogs." They come from Earl Norris and from Norway. "Right now we are not allowed to race with not registered dogs like the Alaska husky." In

Claire and Jacques Philip. Jim Brown photo.

November 1985 they were training for speed races in a beautiful forest near Fontainebleau, France. They are anticipating "good results" as her husband has always been among the top teams in Europe. Their nearby forest trails are a hard packed sand which allows them to use a three-wheeled cart for training when there is no snow.

Jacques is a recent medical school graduate. During the 1985 race he used his training to help Jerry Austin after Austin broke several fingers. He fashioned a splint for Austin's use, and Austin completed the race.

Claire is basically a quiet person. But she is a very warm and friendly person. She is able to openly express her feelings. Along the trail, if something was bothering her, she would come out and tell people what her feelings were.

Claire spends full time at home taking care of their dogs which are like family to her. She used to work for Elan Sport, owned by her father, before she and Jacques started building their sled dog family.

The Philips plan to race the Iditarod again in 1987. Their plans to race in 1986 were postponed due to a lack of the kind of sponsorship they needed to compete again so soon. Her husband plans to come back to Alaska during the 1986 Iditarod to find some more dogs for their next Iditarod race. In the meantime, Claire keeps herself busy providing love and superb care to their family of about 30 dogs. She is indeed an asset to the world of dog mushing.

MONIQUE BENE

Monique Bene, of Coulomiers, France, became the first musher from France to sign up for the Iditarod race. After 23 days on the trail she arrived triumphantly in Nome in 40th position to claim the red lantern as last place finisher in the 1985 Iditarod race.

"During all my life I'll never forget the arrival in Nome. It was really fantas-

Monique Bene arriving at Nome finish line. Jim Brown photo.

tic and the people were so nice. My best souvenir is this red lantern which is in my office."

Her trail to Nome brought her face to face with the meaning of wilderness travel about 100 miles into the race. Confronted by a moose seeking the easier travel afforded by the trail, her progress was temporarily halted. She notes:

"Then he looked at me and came toward me.

"I jumped off the sled. There were trees on the side of the trail, and I thought perhaps I could go on the other side of trees.

"But I fell down on the side of the trail. He came and stayed over me . . . . I had to move my head to see what he was doing. He came back every time I moved a little.

"I thought I was going to die. I thought it would be such a bad way to die, killed by a moose."[5]

After being pinned against the snow for 20 minutes, with the ski mask twisted over her eyes as she fell, the moose finally left. Bene lost no time seeking the protection of the trees. After ascertaining the moose's departure, she walked along the trail hoping to find her dogs who had taken off with her sled. After a two-hour search she found them. They were glad to see her. Fortune smiled on her. As shaken as she was, only one dog had to be dropped at Rabbit Lake because of injury.[6]

Among her cherished memories of the race are the way her dogs performed along the trail. She was impressed by their courage and what they did for her. Her team was composed of dogs she owned as well as dogs she rented. All of the dogs that she owned completed the trip to Nome, in spite of having had less training than the dogs she rented. She feels it is a love story between her dogs and herself.

Looking back on the race, Bene notes that it was such a fantastic experience that she will never forget it. There were many wonderful happenings as she made her way to Nome. There was the sight of "a big flannel with my name" as she arrived in Nikolai. A lady in Koyuk is remembered for all the cakes she made for the women mushers. The stay in McGrath brings back thoughts of the sisters of St. Joseph, and Madeline Dubois and Francis Mitchell who became her friends. She stayed a few restful days in Nome with Karlene and Nick Lemon. The collage of wonderful memories will last forever.

The "biggest anxieties" for her along the trail were the moose attack, the arrival in Shaktoolik, and Norton Sound. She compares her arrival in Shaktoolik as being "like coming to the devil." (The notorious blowing ground storms in that area have been known to do in many mushers in the past.)

Bene's love of sled dogs and mushing was sparked during stopovers in Alaska as a stewardess. Eight years ago she purchased a Siberian husky to take home to France when she quit her airline job. That dog, Moulouk, was not much of a sled dog, preferring to sit in front of the sled rather than pull it. Moulouk was part of her first team, and mushed on her maiden sled dog experience in France. Moulouk is no longer a sled dog. Now he's a cherished pet. But he launched modern sled dog racing in France.[7]

In 1978 following a sprint run in the hill region of Jura, the "Club de la Pulka et du Traineau a Chiens" came into existence. (English translation is the Pulka and Dog Sled Club.) The pulka is a small toboggan pulled by a single dog accompanied by a skier. This type of outfit is also commonly used in the Scandinavian countries. The Pulka Club has grown immensely. Now numbering over 300 members, sprint races are held every week in the winter. Its first long distance race, an 80-kilometer event, was first held in 1984. However, most races are no longer than 18 miles.[7]

Bene, who lives near Paris, France, returned to Alaska every two to three months prior to the race to purchase purebred Siberian huskies and train with Natalie and Earl Norris of the Howling Dog Farm at Willow. In 1984 bright yellow posters began appearing in Paris showing a map of Alaska and the slogan "IDITAROD la plus llonge course au monde de TRAINEAUX A CHIENS." Seeking sponsors for the 1985 Iditarod, Bene found businesses were reluctant to commit themselves.[7]

Bene was born at the frontier between France, Switzerland and Germany in 1950. She has one brother, five years younger. However, there were no dogs in the family and she missed having one very much.

She studied at Strasbourg University where she obtained a public relations diploma. She spent five years as an airline stewardess.

In 1974 she married an airline pilot. She has two daughters, eight-year-old Aude Gaelle and five-year-old Johanne. Aude Gaelle loves huskies and is so proud of her mother that she wants to follow mother's footsteps. She wanted to sleep outside in a tent in the summer of 1985, like her mother did along the trail. She has her own Siberian whom she harnesses up and has haul a small cart. Soon she will have a small sled of her own for her dog.

Bene's husband did not share her love for huskies and sled dog races, and their marriage dissolved in 1984. Now Monique feels she is able to have a real musher's life.

Bene's kennel has 28 purebred Siberians, plus eight puppies born in December 1985. She plans to make two open category sled dog teams. One team is for her own use and the other team will be driven by her boyfriend, Patrick Guillaud. He shares her love of dogs and the outdoor life. Both Bene and Guillaud would like to race in the 1987 Iditarod. However, she notes she will need to find more sponsors than she had in 1985. Otherwise she feels she will have to forget the idea. (It cost her about $40,000 to run the 1985 race.)

At Rainy Pass, after coming down into Happy Valley, Bene arrived "bumped, bruised, banged and broken." She then told race marshall Donna Gentry, "Now I can call myself true Alaskan dog musher."[78] She indeed is a true Alaskan musher, having experienced both the pleasures and perils of the Alaskan wilderness and the Iditarod.

Monique Bene. Photo courtesy of M. Bene.

LES HUSKIES SIBÉRIENS de POINT-BARROW

Elevage Amateur

Monique BENE
Iditarod Finisher

Moulouk. Photo courtesy of M. Bene.

CHAPTER 7

1986 Entrants

Several women mushers have signed up early for the 1986 Iditarod. These include Susan Butcher, Kari Skogen, and Pat Danly. Others planning to run include Fritz Kirsch and newcomer Nina Hotvedt of Andebu, Norway. If Hotvedt runs, there will be two women racers from Norway in the 1986 Iditarod as Skogen is also from Norway.

PAT DANLEY

Pat Danly and her husband, Bill Hall, have both entered the 1986 Iditarod. Her interest in dog driving began in 1975 when she and Bill moved to Eagle River, Alaska. They began "accumulating" dogs about two years later. She used to ski a lot, and had traveled extensively since graduating with a Bachelor of Fine Arts from Stevens College in Columbia, Missouri. "Dogs seemed the best way to get around and see the country."

Beginning in 1978 she and her husband became involved with the Iditarod race as amateur radio operators, volunteering at various checkpoints: 1978 at Skwentna; 1979 at Skwentna, Rohn River, and Shageluk; 1980-1981 at Finger Lake; and 1982 at Rohn River. The first two years they flew to their checkpoints. From 1980-1982 they both drove their teams into their checkpoints carrying radio equipment, generator and battery. Mushing was "preferable to flying in!"

In 1978 she purchased her first good puppy from Patty Friend and Rod Perry with the intention of someday running the race. She and her husband have always maintained separate dog lots. The cost of maintaining their dogs led them to want to race. So far all the dogs in her 1986 race team are related to that puppy who is her lead dog.

In 1983 Pat and her husband quit their jobs as computer programmers, sold their Eagle River cabin, and moved to Trapper Creek. There they are able to run dogs right out of their back door and seriously train.

The 1985-1986 racing season is the first time that they have had enough dogs to field two teams. Due to expense and team quality reasons, she feels it would be best to run one team with the best dogs from each of their lots. But each of them wants to go and doesn't want to prevent the other from going. "A flip of the coin didn't work. So we're both going this year." They hope to get most of their dogs there, "see what we've got, and learn the way." After the race they will probably cut down their dog lot size by keeping only the best dogs, and take turns running in future Iditarods.

Danly has raced the "fun" races in Trapper Creek. In the sprints she came in 1st, 2nd and 4th. She also ran the Moose Creek 200 last year. The starts and crowds bother her a lot, and make her nervous. Once she is out on the trail she again becomes comfortable. She likes to travel alone — out of sight of her husband — but does hope to camp together now and then with him on the Iditarod. "Bill's my favorite camping buddy." The two don't mind competing against each other. "The dogs are basically the same so whoever does best we both share in it — but here's hoping I beat Bill!"

This rookie Iditarod musher grew up in the Chicago area, the oldest in a family of five. Her folks now live in Charlevoux, Michigan, where she spent summers. She used to sail summers on the Great Lakes, and still does when visiting her family.

Now firmly an Alaskan, she will be 35 when she starts the 1986 Iditarod. She and Bill have no children and have no plans for any, and she feels, "The dogs are like our kids." Thus she and Bill and their "family" of dogs will be on the trail experiencing the peace and beauty as well as the challenge of long distance dog team racing along the historic Iditarod Trail.

NINA HOTVEDT

Nina Hotvedt, a 21-year-old musher from Andebu, Norway, plans to be in the starting lineup in the 1986 Iditarod. Her interest and excitement about the Iditarod were sparked by the 1983 race when Roger Legaard, a Norwegian and member of the dog mushing group she belongs to, competed in the Iditarod race. (Legaard placed 10th and obtained "Rookie of the Year" honors.)

Hotvedt enjoys mountain climbing and glacier walking. On excursions to the mountains she often took her Siberian husky. At age 15 she began dog mushing, Nordic style (traveling behind the sled on skis). She has always enjoyed the outdoors life.

A determined, independent person, Hotvedt first came to Alaska in the summer of 1983. Although she did not know anyone in Alaska, she carried a list of people and telephone numbers provided by Roger Legaard. When she telephoned Chris Moore of the Iditaski (a cross country ski race on the Iditarod Trail) and others, she found Alaskans very hospitable.[1]

She is impressed by the vastness of the Alaskan wilderness, and especially the long distances one can travel without encountering small towns. In Norway she was used to finding homes or small towns at closer intervals than one finds in some of the vast Alaska wilderness. She finds her stay here very interesting, and feels that she learns something new every day.

After doing a little traveling and getting a bit acquainted with Alaska, she heard that Burt Bomhoff needed a dog handler at his Trapper Creek training camp. She landed the job, and spent nearly five months there, working with his dogs until a few days before the 1985 Iditarod.

While in Nome during the 1985

Nina Hotvedt and lead dog Ophir. Ron Wendt photo, courtesy of Nina Hotvedt.

race she talked to Joe Redington Sr. She made a deal with him to use some of his dogs for the 1986 race. Part of the time since then she lived at his dog lot, getting acquainted with his dogs. Much time has been spent busily working at securing sponsors and doing all the myriad tasks necessary to enter the race. Dave and Donna Olson provided her with an aluminum sled for training, and she had a special toboggan sled built for her by Ed Bordon for use in the 1986 Iditarod.

Hotvedt is particularly appreciative of the support she has received from Frances and Lars Vadla of Big Lake who have allowed her to live with them while training in the area, and to Penny and Vern Cherneski who have allowed her to keep her dogs at their lot. She gives thanks to all her friends back home in Norway for "great support," and to her friends in Alaska and the "lower 48" for their support in making it possible to train for the 1986 Iditarod.

Hotvedt has a brother four years her senior. Her father is in the banking business, and her mother is a hairdresser.

After the 1986 Iditarod she plans to further her education. Although her career plans are not yet firmly decided, she is strongly considering the field of teaching physical education. Until she returns to Norway she will be pursuing her own dreams and adventures in preparing for and racing along the Iditarod trail.

When these women mushers take to the trail in the 1986 Iditarod, they will be adding to the tradition and record of the 29 mushers who ran between 1974 and 1985. Twenty-five of those 29 have completed the race at least once, and these 29 women have run a total of 49 times, finishing 40 times. Their record indicates that they have been able to compete on an equal footing with the men, and they have a higher percentage of race completions than the men. Perhaps their determination has been greater than their male counterparts to prove that they indeed can meet the tests of mother nature and Alaskan conditions along the historic Iditarod Trail.

However, Libby Riddles, 1985 Iditarod champion, will not be among the women running in the 1986 Iditarod. It is Joe Garnie's turn (her partner) to race their jointly-owned team in the 1986 race.

Iditarod Race Statistics

1973
37 racers started
23 racers finished
No women entered

1974
44 racers started
26 racers finished
Mary Shields — 23rd
Lolly Medley — 24th

1975
41 racers started
25 racers finished
Ginger Burcham — scratched

1976
47 racers started
34 racers finished
No women entered the race

1977
49 racers started
36 racers finished
Varona Thompson — 34th
Dinah Knight — scratched

1978
39 racers started
34 racers finished
Susan Butcher — 19th
Varona Thompson — 20th
Shelley Vandiver (Gill) — 29th

1979
55 racers started
47 racers finished
Susan Butcher — 9th
Patty Friend — 20th

1980
61 racers started
36 racers finished
Susan Butcher — 5th
Donna Gentry — 10th
Libby Riddles — 18th
Dee Dee Jonrowe — 24th
Marjorie Moore — 30th
Barbara Moore — 36th
Varona Thompson — scratched

1981
53 racers started
38 racers finished
Susan Butcher — 5th
Donna Gentry — 18th
Libby Riddles — 20th
Dee Dee Jonrowe — 31st
Sue Firmin — 32nd

1982
54 racers started
46 racers finished
Susan Butcher — 2nd
Rose Albert — 32nd
Sue Firmin — scratched

1983
68 racers started
54 racers finished
Susan Butcher — 9th
Sue Firmin — 14th
Dee Dee Jonrowe — 15th
Roxy Wright — 23rd
Shannon Poole — 29th
Christine O'Gar — 32nd
Connie Frerichs — 39th
Fritz Kirsch — 48th
Pam Flowers — 51st
Beverly Jerue — scratched

1984
67 racers started
45 racers finished
Susan Butcher — 2nd
Diana Dronenburg — 27th
Sue Firmin — 28th
Dee Dee Jonrowe — 30th
Kari Skogen — 35th
Francine Bennis — 38th
Miki Collins — scratched
Connie Frerichs — scratched
Lolly Medley — scratched

1985
61 racers started
40 racers finished
Libby Riddles — 1st
Betsy McGuire — 29th
Claire Philip — 37th
Monique Bene — 40th
Susan Butcher — scratched

Footnotes

CHAPTER 1

1. "The Iditarod National Historic Trail: Seward to Nome Route," Vol. 1, A Comprehensive Management Plan, September 1981, (Anchorage:BLM) p. 19.
2. Ibid.
3. Michael E. Smith, *Alaska's Historic Roadhouses*, (The Alaska Division of Parks, Office of History and Archaeology, 1972) p. 38.
4. Kenneth A. Ungermann, *The Race to Nome*, (Harper & Row, c. 1963) A Breakthrough Book, p. 165.
5. Ibid, p. 164.
6. W.L. Goodwin, "Report of the Winter Reconnaissance, Seward to Nome," letter to Alaska Road Commission, dated April 16, 1908, p. 1.
7. Charles Lee Cadwallader, *Reminiscences of the Iditarod Trail*, no date, pp. 6-9.
8. S. Hall Young, *Adventures in Alaska*, (New York: Fleming H. Revell Co., 1919), pp. 80-81.
9. Ibid, p. 88.
10. Ibid, p. 91.
11. Ibid, p. 93.
12. Ibid, p. 99.
13. Hudson Stuck, *Ten Thousand Miles with a Dog Sled*, (New York: Charles Scribner's Sons, c. 1914, 1916) 2nd edition, 1917, pp. 139-140.
14. Ibid, p. 321.
15. Goodwin, op. cit., p. 7.
16. Ibid, p. 10.
17. Ibid, p. 11.
18. Smith, op. cit., p. 38.

CHAPTER 2

1. Esther Birdsall Darling, "The Great Dog Races of Nome," ca. 1916, reprinted by Iditarod Trail Committee, Knik, AK, 1969, no page numbers.
2. *Iditarod Trail Annual 1979*, p. 35.
3. *Iditarod Trail Annual 1981*, p. 35.
4. *Iditarod Pioneer*, January 17, 1914, p. 3.
5. *Iditarod Pioneer*, January 10, 1914, p. 4.
6. Betsy Hart, *The History of Ruby, Alaska "The Gem of the Yukon,"* (National Bilingual Materials Development Center, University of Alaska, Anchorage), p. 30.
7. Interview with Rose Albert, October 6, 1985.
8. Earl Norris, "History of Modern Sled Dog Racing in Alaska," *Racing Alaska Sled Dogs*, compiled by Bill Vaudrin (Anchorage: Alaska Northwest Publishing Company, c. 1976), p. 18.
9. *Iditarod Trail Annual 1974*, p. 10.
10. Recollections of Vi Redington, December 1985.
11. Race Statistics in Vaudrin's *Racing Alaskan Sled Dogs*, op. cit., p. 109.
12. Ungermann, op. cit., p. 165.
13. *Iditarod Trail Annual 1974*, p. 20.
14. Ibid, p. 45.
15. *Iditarod Trail Annual 1978*, p. 82.
16. Shannon Garst, *Scotty Allan, King of the Dog Team Drivers*, (New York: Julian Messner, Inc., c. 1946), p. 201.
17. Esther Birdsall Darling, *Baldy of Nome*, (Philadelphia: The Penn Publishing Company, c. 1916, 1920), p. 299.
18. Garst, op. cit., pp. 214-216.
19. *Alaska Magazine*, April 1974, p. A-15.

CHAPTER 3

1. Mary Shields, *Sled Dog Trails*, (Anchorage: Alaska Northwest Publishing Company, 1984), p. 6.
2. Ibid, pp. 36-37.
3. Ibid, p. 45.

CHAPTER 4

1. Susan Butcher, "A Woman's Struggle: Thousand-Mile Race to Nome," *National Geographic*, v. 163:3, March 1983, p. 414.
2. Ibid.
3. Ibid, p. 415.
4. Ibid, p. 420.
5. Ibid, p. 420, 422.
6. Ibid, p. 422.
7. Susan Butcher, "Butcher relives trail tragedy," *The Anchorage Times*, March 8, 1985, p. E-9.
8. Ibid, pp. E-9 and E-10.
9. Ibid, p. E-10.

10. Chris Fortenberry, "Butcher-Monson 'Harnessed,'" *The Iditarod Runner*, v. 9:1 October 1985, pp. 4-5, conversation with Gene Gilman.
11. *Anchorage Daily News, Iditarod 1985*, (News Books International, Inc., Indianapolis, Indiana, 1985), p. 74.
12. Ibid, p. 75.
13. Libby Riddles, speech at Valley Women's Resource Center, "An Evening with Libby Riddles," Wasilla, Alaska, October 18, 1985.
14. *Anchorage Daily News, Iditarod 1985*, op. cit., p. 78.
15. Ibid, p. 82.
16. Ibid, p. 90.
17. Libby Riddles, October 18, 1985.
18. *The Anchorage Times*, August 22, 1985, Extra Final Edition, p. 1.
19. Carol A. Phillips, "The Longest Trip Home," *Alaska Magazine*, March 1981, p. 31.
20. Ibid, pp. 59-60.
21. Ibid, pp. 60-61.

CHAPTER 6

1. Miki Collins, "Mushing Against the Winds," *Alaska Airlines Magazine*, March 1985, p. 34.
2. Ibid, p. 32.
3. Ibid, p. 33.
4. Susan Carroll, "French Mushers Challenge Iditarod," 1985 *Frontiersman* Iditarod Issue, p. 7.
5. David Foster, "French find new hazard: The moose," *Anchorage Daily News*, March 12, 1985, p. B-1.
6. Ibid, p. B-3.
7. Joe Bridgeman, " 'Iditarod Spirit' targets France," reprinted from *The Anchorage Times* in *The Iditarod Runner*, v. 7:6, September 1984, p. 9.
8. Interview with Donna Gentry.

CHAPTER 7

1. Susan Carroll, "Norwegian woman gets headstart on '86 Iditarod race, *The Frontiersman*, May 4, 1985, p. 10.

Bibliography

Anchorage Daily News, *Iditarod 1985: 13th Annual Anchorage-to-Nome Trail Sled Dog Race*, News Books International Inc., Indianapolis, Indiana, 1985.

Andrews, C. L., *The Story of Alaska*, The Caxton Printers, Ltd., Caldwell, Idaho, ©1938.

Attla, George, *The Iditarod: The Most Demanding Race of All*, as told to Bella Levorsen, Arner Publications, Rome, New York, ©1974, 2nd edition.

Bridgeman, Joe, "Iditarod Spirit" Targets France, *The Iditarod Runner*, September 1984.

Butcher, Susan, "A Woman's Struggle: Thousand-Mile Race to Nome, *National Geographic*, March 1983.

Butcher, Susan, "Butcher relives trail tragedy," *The Anchorage Times*, March 8, 1985.

Cadwallader, Charles, *Reminiscences of the Iditarod Trail*, no date.

Carroll, Susan, "French Mushers Challenge Iditarod," *Frontiersman*, 1985 Iditarod issue.

Carroll, Susan, "Norwegian woman gets headstart on '86 Iditarod race," *The Frontiersman*, May 4, 1985.

Colby, Merle, (Federal Writers Project) *A Guide to Alaska*, The Macmillan Company, New York, 1936.

Collins, Miki, "Mushing Against the Winds," *Alaska Airlines Magazine*, March 1985.

Darling, Esther Birdsall, *Baldy of Nome*, The Penn Publishing Company, Philadelphia, ©1916, 1920.

Darling, Esther Birdsall, *The Great Dog Races of Nome*, Official Souvenir History, ©1916, reprinted by Iditarod Trail Committee, Knik, Alaska, 1969.

Foster, David, "French find new hazard: the Moose," *Anchorage Daily News*, March 12, 1985.

Garst, Shannon, *Scotty Allan, King of the Dog Team Drivers*, Julian Messner, Inc., New York City, ©1946.

Goodwin, W. L., letter of April 16, 1908, describing a winter reconnaissance from Seward to Nome, January 31 to April 5, 1908, to the Alaska Road Commission.

Hart, Betsy, *The History of Ruby, Alaska, "The Gem of the Yukon,"* National Bilingual Development Center, Anchorage, Alaska, no date.

Hulley, Clarence C., *Alaska, Past and Present*, Binfords & Mort, Portland, Oregon, 1958 revision.

Iditarod Trail Committee, *Iditarod Press Packet*, 1985.

Jones, Tim, *The Last Great Race*, Madronna Publishers, Seattle, 1982.

Levorson, Bella, *Mush · A Beginner's Manual of Sled Dog Training*, Arner Publications, Westmoreland, New York, ©1976, 3rd printing.

McLain, Carrie, *Gold Rush Nome*, Graphic Arts Center, Portland, Oregon, ©1969.

Page, Dorothy, *Iditarod Trail Annual, Anchorage to Nome Race*, 1974-1985 editions.

Phillips, Carol A., "The Longest Trip Home," *Alaska Magazine*, March 1981.

Potter, Lousie, *Old Times on Upper Cook Inlet*, Book Cache, Anchorage, 1967.

Ricker, Elizabeth M., *Seppala: Alaska Dog Driver*, Little, Brown & Co., Boston, 1930.

Shields, Mary, *Sled Dog Trails*, Alaska Northwest Publishing Co., Anchorage, 1984.

Smith, Michael, *Alaska's Roadhouses*, WICHE, Alaska Division of Parks, Office of History and Archeology.

Souvenir of Second All Alaska Sweepstakes, Nome, Alaska, April 1, 1909, ©1909 by George S. Maynard, reprinted by the Iditarod Trail Committee, Knik, Alaska, 1969.

Stuck, Hudson, *Ten Thousand Miles with a Dog Sled*, Charles Scribner's Sons, New York, ©1914, 1916, 2nd edition 1927.

Stuck, Hudson, *Voyages on the Yukon and its Tributaries*, Charles Scribner's Sons, New York, 1917.

Ungerman, Kenneth A., *The Race to Nome*, Harper & Row, New York, ©1963.

U.S. Dept. of Interior, BLM, "The Iditarod National Historic Trail, Seward to Nome Route, Vol. I, A Comprehensive Management Plan," 1981.

Vandiver, Shelley, Gill, "Women who run the Iditarod," *Alaskan Women*, Vol 1:1, March 1982.

Vaudrin, Bill, *Racing Alaskan Sled Dogs*, Alaska Northwest Publishing Co., Anchorage, Alaska, ©1976, 2nd printing.

Young, S. Hall, *Adventures in Alaska*, Fleming H. Revell Company, New York, ©1919.

Interviews and correspondence with the women mushers profiled in this book:

The Alaska Magazine

The Anchorage Daily News

The Anchorage Times

The Frontiersman and *Valley Sun* newspapers, Palmer and Wasilla, Alaska.

The Iditarod Pioneer

The Iditarod Runner, official newsletter of the Iditarod Trail Committee.

Glossary

ALASKAN HUSKY Any arctic or northern breed with heavy double coat, curly tail.

ALASKAN MALEMUTE Large northern dog breed recognized by the American Kennel Club.

BASKET The part of the sled which holds the passenger or load.

BOOTIES A kind of cloth sock made to protect the dog's feet from small cuts and sores.

BRAKE A pronged piece of metal fastened to a board fastened to the sled, held by a spring. Used to slow or stop a team.

BRUSH BOW Curved piece of wood around the front of sleds to ward off brush.

CHUTE The starting line and take off area.

DOG BOX Plywood box with compartments on the back of a truck or trailer used to transport dogs.

DOG YARD, LOT OR KENNEL The area near the musher's home where dogs are kept.

DOUBLE LEAD Two lead dogs who lead the team side by side.

GANG LINE, TOW LINE The main line (center line) that runs forward from the sled and to which the dogs are hitched.

GEE! Command for right turn.

HANDLEBAR Loop or driving bow held by the driver.

HAW! Command for left turn.

HIKE! Command to start a dog team moving.

HOOK, SNOW HOOK Sharp pieces of curved metal attached to the sled by a line. Used to hold the team by being embedded in the snow or wrapped around a tree.

INDIAN DOG An Alaskan husky from an Indian village.

LEAD DOG, LEADER Dog who runs in front of the others. Generally must be both intelligent and fast.

MALEMUTE Term used by old time Alaskans for any sled dog.

MUSH!, ALL RIGHT!, LET'S GO!, HIKE! Commands to start a team.

MUSHER The person who drives a dog team.

NECK LINE Line that connects a dog's collar to tow line and between the two collars of a double lead.

OVERFLOW Water on top of a frozen lake.

RUNNERS The surfaces on which sleds slide. May be wood, plastic or steel.

RENDEZVOUS, FUR RENDEZVOUS, "RONDY" A mid-winter festival held in February in Anchorage; begun in 1936. Dog sled races began in 1946. Both Women's Championship races and the major World Championship Race (open to men and women) are held.

SIBERIAN HUSKY A medium size (average 50 pounds) northern dog breed recognized by the American Kennel Club. Often has blue eyes.

SLED BAG A specially made cloth or canvas bag which fits inside the sled basket and zips up to hold mushers gear. Iditarod racers often sleep in it on the trail.

SPRINT RACES Shorter races where speed is important. Generally no more than 25 to 30 miles a day as contrasted to the 200 mile races and the Iditarod race.

STAKE A metal or wooden post driven into the ground to which a dog is tied or chained.

STANCHIONS OR STRUTS The vertical or upright parts of a sled.

SWING DOG(S) Dog(s) directly behind the lead dog. The swing dog(s) job is to help "swing" the team in the turns or curves.

TOW LINE, GANG LINE The main line running forward of the sled to which all the dogs are connected by other lines.

WHEEL DOGS, WHEELERS Dogs directly in front of the sled.

WHOA! A command used to stop or halt the dog team. Usually accompanied by heavy pressure on the brake.

Index

NOTE: Photographs are listed in **bold type**.

Ahmasuk, Harold, 33, 35
Aisenbrey, David, 59
Alaska Central Railway **2**, 4, 6
Alaska Gold Rush, 3
Alaska Historical Library, **10**, **11**
Alaska Purchase Centennial Race, 9, 12
Alaska Railroad, 5, 6, 7
Alaska Range, 6
Alaska Road Commission, 3, 7
Albert, Alice, 11, **11**, 43
Albert, George, 43
Albert, Harvey, 43, 44
Albert, Howard, 43, 44
Albert, Phillip, Sr., 43
Albert, Rose, 11, 14, 41, 43-44, **43**
All Alaska Sweepstakes, 9, **9**, 10, **10**, 30
Allan, "Scotty," 10, 14
American Women's North Pole Expedition, 52
Amethyst (dog), 58, **58**
Anchorage, 5, 7
Anchorage Museum, The, **5**, 12
Anchorage, Open World Championship Sled Dog Race, 12, 18, 37, 44, 45, 62
Anchorage Women's World Championship Sled Dog Race, 18, 36, 44, 45
Ansley, William, **11**
Anvik, 53
Anvik Creek, 4
Anvik River, 35
Anvil Creek, 4, **4**
Arpino, Bill, 19
Attla, George, 12, 46
Aurora Dog Mushers, 12
Austin, Jerry, 26, 63
Axle (dog), 34

Balto (dog), 5
Barve, Lavon, 33
Baumgartner, Ernie, 26
Beargrease, John (see John Beargrease Race)
Beaver Creek Checkpoint, 36
Bender, Col., 13
Bene, Monique 14, 55, 62, 63-64, **63**, **64**
Bennis, Francine, 57-59, **58**
Berger, J., 10
Bering Coast, 4, 32
Bering Sea, 4
Bethel, 35, 36
Big River Roadhouse, 6

Birchwood, 30
Bomhoff, Burt, 66
Bonanza, 7
Bonanza Roadhouse, 7
Boots, **38**, 39
Boyer, Dennis, 35
Bristol Bay, 35, 36, 58, 59
Brown, Jim **17**, **22**, **26**, **30**, **33**, **34**, **35**, **36**, **40**, **41**, **45**, **49**, **57**, **62**, **63**
Bryar, Jean, 31
Buckle, Mike, 38
Bulls Eye — Angel Creek Race, 47, 53
Burcham, Ginger, 13, 15, 18-19, **18**
Bureau of Land Management (BLM), 3, 30, 32, 33, 53
Burnham, Richard, 19
Buster (Alec Brown's lead dog), 11
Butcher, Susan, 13, 14, 20, **22**, 23-27, **23**, **25**, 33, 35, 36, 39, 41, 55, 65
Byrd, Admiral Richard (1928 Antarctic Expedition), 51

Cabbage (dog), 15-16
Cadwallader, Charles Lee, 6, 7
Candle, 9
Canton's Pioneer Roadhouse, **5**
Carlson, Slim, 59
Carney, Ed, 12
Carroll, Susan, 62
Carter, Landon, 38
Champaine, Charlie, 45
Chase, Ken, 17, 52
Chena Hot Springs, 53
Cherneski, Penny, 66
Cherneski, Vern, 66
Chugiak, 29, 30
Clinton, Ed, 28
Clough's Roadhouse (McGrath Roadhouse), **6**
Cold Foot Classic, 27, 47
Collins, Julie, 59, 60
Collins, Miki, 59-60, **59**
Cook Inlet, 4
Cooper, John, 34
Council, 10
Cripple Checkpoint, 55, 59
Crisman, Dennis, 46
Crow Pass, 6
Cruickshank, John, 30

D&D Kennels, 56
Dalzel Canyon, 59
Dalzell River, 6
Danley, Pat, 65
David Walluk Race, 39
Dawson, 4

Delzene, Fay, 10
Demoski, Rudy, 33, 52
Dillingham Corporation, 45
Diphtheria serum dog team run, 5, 12
Dishakaket, 6
Dobbs, B.B., **9**, **10**
Don's Iditarod 200, 62
Dronenburg, Diana, 55-56, **55**
Dronenburg, John, 56
Dronenburg, Ray, 55, 56
Dubois, Madeline, 64
Dugan (dog), 34

Eagle Island, 33
Eagle River, 6
Earhart, Shannon, 45
Egypt Mountain, 31
Eklutna, 6
Elim, 61
Ellingson, Dinah (see Knight, Dinah)
Ellingson, Ron, 21
Evans, Charles, 5

Fairbanks, 4, 5, 16, 47, 48, 53, 59
Fairbanks Daily News Miner, **15**, 17
Fairbanks North American Dog Sled Race (Open), 44
Fairbanks Women's North American Sled Dog Race, 18, 44
Farewell, 38
Farewell Burn, 25, 31-32, 33, 50, 51
Farewell Lake, 35, 52
Farley, Howard, 13
Findlay, Glenn, 26
Finger Lake, 18, 36, 53, 65
Fink, Albert, 10
Firmin, Bill, 41, 42
Firmin, Sue, 13, 14, 35, 36, **40**, 41-43, **41**
Firmin, Theresa, 42
Fitka, Charlie, 24
Flat, 11
Flat Creek, **2**
Flat Horn Lake, 12, 42
Flowers, Pam, 51-52, **51**
Folger, Andy, 43
French Joe's Roadhouse, 6
Frerichs, Connie, **22**, 48-49, **48**
Friend, Patty, 13, 24, 28, 29-30, **30**, 32, 65
Fritz's Roadhouse, 6

Galena, 16, 38, 55
Ganes Creek, 3, 6
Garnie, Joe, 33, 34, 35
Gavin, Shirley, 12

71

Genet, Ray, 25
Gentry, Donna, 13, 23, 31-32, **31**, 33, 41, 62, 64
Gill, Shelley (Vandiver), 13, 27-29, **28**
Glacier Creek, 4, 6
Golden Harness Award, 17
Golovin, 38
Golovin Bay, 7
Goodwin, W.L., 3, 4, 5, 6, 7
Goose Bay, 20, 24, 25
Granite (dog), 26, 27
Guillaud, Patrick, 64

Haas, Rene, 14
Halfway Roadhouse (Shermier Roadhouse), 6
Hall, Bill, 65
Halverson, Duane "Dewey," 26, 32, 33, 34, 47
Happy River, 6
Happy River Roadhouse, 6
Happy Valley, 64
Hegness, John, 9
Hoe, Mari, 58
Hope, 4
Hotvedt, Nina, 65, 66
Hughes, Lynette, 45
Huntington, Carl, 13, 16

Iditarod, 3-7, 11
Iditarod District, 5
Iditarod Kennel Club, 11
Iditarod Ladies' Race, 11, **11**
Iditarod Race Sportsmanship Trophy, 35-36
Iditarod Sweepstakes, 11
Iditarod Trail Committee, 25, 27, 31, 34, 36, 42
Iditaski, 66
Innoko District, 4, 6
Innoko River, 7, 59
Iron Dog Snowmobile Race, 53
Ivak (dog), 24

Jerue, Beverly (see Masek, Beverly)
Jerue, Carl, 53
Jerue, Marie, 53
Jimmie, George, 11
John Beargrease Race, 27, 35, 36
Johnson, John, 10
Jones, Gloria, 12
Jones, Kathy, **22**
Jonrowe, Dee Dee, 13, 14, 23, 35-36, **35**, 42
Jonrowe, Mike, 36

Kaiyuk Slough, 6
Kallands, Edgar, 5
Kaltag, 6, 7, 19, 20, 36

Kaltag Portage, 3
Kemp Pacific Fisheries, 35
Khatchikian, Armen, 57
King, Al, 4
Kirsch, Fritz, 49-50, **49**, 65
Klondike Gold Rush, 4
Knight, Dinah, 13, 15, 21, **21**
Knik, **5**, 6, 24, 28
Knik Arm, 4, 6
Knik Kennels, 49
Kojima, Kazuo, 49
Kokrines, 11, 43
Kottke, Joel, 42
Koyuk, 34, 36, 37, 46, 48, 64
KSKO McGrath, 61
Kusko 300, 27, 34, 35, 36, 42
Kuskokwim River, 6, 59

Laconia World Sled Dog Race, 31
Lake Minchumina, 59, 60
Lakeview, 6
Lang, Carla, 28
Lang, Ray, 28
Lauwer, Calvin, 57
Lee, Bobby, 50
Legaard, Roger, 66
Lemon, Karlene, 64
Lemon, Nick, 64
Leonard, Gene, 49, 53
Leonard, June, 53
Lindner, Sonny, 10, 36, 39, 48
Little Susitna Roadhouse, 6
Lomen Bros., **2**
Long City, 11

Mackey, Dick, 13, 14, 17, 20, 58, 61
Mackey, Rick, 14, 36
McCarty, Bill, 5
McGrath, 5, 7, 13, 49, 52, 59, 60, 61, 64
McGrath Mail Trail 200, 60, 61
McGrath Roadhouse, 6, **6**
McGuire, Betsy, 60-62, **60**
McKinley, Mt. dog team ascent, 23, 25
McKinley Park, 15
Manley, 28
Martinique, Susan, 19
Masek, Beverly Jerue, 52-53, **52**
Masek, Jan, 52, 53
Masek, Michael Jan Albert, 53
May, Joe, 13
Medley, Lolly, 13, 15-18, **15**, 49
Miller, Rusty, 47
Mitchell, Francis, **59**, 64
Monson, David, 27
Moore, Barbara, 13, 37-39, **38**
Moore, Carla, 39
Moore, Chris, 66
Moore, Lew, 36
Moore, Lisa, 37, 38, **38**, 39

Moore, Marjorie Ann, 13, 36-37, **37**
Moose Creek 200, 65
Moses Point, 61
Mountain Climbers Roadhouse, 6
Murkowski, Frank, 53
Musk Oxen, 23, 24, 47

Nayokupuk, Herbie, 26
Nelchina, 33
Nenana, 5, 7
New England Sled Dog Racing Association, 32
… Club Trophy, 32
Nielsen, Nicki, **2**, **4**, **6**, **7**, **8**, **9**, **19**, 55
Nielsen, Robert, **14**, **23**, **31**, **43**, **46**, **58**, **60**
Nikolai, 7, 31, 38, 48, 59, 60, 61, 64
Nine Mile Hill, 24
Nollner, Edgar, 5
Nome, 3-7, 9, 10, 16, 17, 34, 38, 39, **54**, 56, 58, 60, 61
Nome Kennel Club, 9, 10, **13**, 14
Norris, Earl, 41, 51, 56, 57, 62, 64
Norris, Natalie, 51, 58, 59, 62, 64
North American Sled Dog Race Championship Races (see Fairbanks North American Sled Dog Races)
Norton Sound, 64
Nulato, 3

O'Gar, Christine, 47-48, **47**
O'Gar, Henry, 48
O'Gar, Marion, 48
Okleasik, Issac, 12, 39
Olson, Dave, 13, 33, 36, 66
Olson, Donna, 66
Ophir, 3, 6, 31, 59, 61
Ophir Creek, 6
Ophir Roadhouse, 6
Osmar, Dean, 14

Page, Dorothy, 12
Palmer, Walt, 35
Paniptchuk, Saul, 51
Pass Creek, 6
Peluk Roadhouse, 6
Perry, Alan 32
Perry, Rod, 29, 30, 32, 65
Peters, Edna, 53
Peters, Emmitt, 13, 18, 26, 53
Peterson, Will, 61
Philip, Claire, 14, 55, 62-63, **62**
Philip, Jacques, 14, 62, 63
Phillips, Rosemary, 20, **21**
Pioneer Roadhouse (**Canton's**), 5
Pioneer Roadhouse (French Joe's), 6
Poole, Eric, 46, 47
Poole, Shannon, 45-47, **46**
Ptarmigan Lake (Wrangell Mts.), 24

72

Ptarmigan Pass, 16, 18
Pup Pup (dog), 31-32, **31**

Rabbit Lake, 26, 27, 60, 63
Rainy Pass, 6, 28, 31, 36, 37, **46**, 52, 56, 64
Rainy Pass Lodge, 55
Rainy Pass Roadhouse, 6
Ramsey, Fox (Col), 9, 10
Reagan, Ronald, 53
Redington, Joe, Jr., 28
Redington, Joe, Sr., 12, **12**, 13, 23, 24, 25, 28, 30, 39, 49, 58, 60, 62, 66
Redington, Vi, 12
Red Lantern, 20, **38**
Resurrection Bay, 4
Resurrection Creek, 4
Rhone River Roadhouse, 6, 31, 55
Richardson, Maj. Wilds P., 4
Riddles, Libby, 13, 14, 19, 23, 27, 28, 30, 32-35, **33**, **34**, 41, **54**, 55
Riddles, Mary, 33, 34
Riddles, Willard, 34
Rieger, Steve, 56
Riley, Jerry, 13, 29, 30
Roberts, "Robby," 59
Rohn, 59
Rohn River, 20, 33, 35, 44, 50, 52, 65
Ruby, 3, 5, 11, 43
Ruby Derby, 11, **11**
Ruegg, Lt. Gen., 13

Safety, 32, 34, 38, 58
Salmon River Roadhouse, 6
Sampson, Frank 36
Schultz, Jeff, **54**
Schultz, John, 13
Seamore, Dolly, 17
Seppala, Leonhard, 5, 10, 11, 12
Serum Run (1925), 5
Seward, 3, 4, 5, 6, 7
Shageluk, 36, 65

Shaktoolik, 7, 33, 34, 36, 37, 38, 46, 48, 55, 61, 64
Shepard, Pete, 12
Shermier Roadhouse, 6
Shields, Mary, 13, 15-16, **15**, 17
Skagway, 4
Skogen, Kari, 14, 55, 56-57, **57**, 65
Skwentna, 25, 65
Skwentna Crossing Roadhouse, 6
Skwentna River, 6
Smyth, Bud 17
Solomon, 10, 11, 34
Sportsmanship Trophy, 36
Spude, Robert L, 3
Steamer Corwin, **7**
Stevens, Ted, 53
Stuck, Hudson, 7
Sunder, Bob, 59
Sunrise, 4
Susitna River, 4, 6
Susitna Roadhouse, 6
Susitna Station, 6, 7, 13
Swenson, Rick, 10, 13, 14, 25, 27, 28, 35, 36, 39, 41

Takotna, 6, 59, 60
Takotna River, 6
Takotna Roadhouse, 6
Takotna Slough, 6
Tang (dog), 49
Teegarden, Jim, 46
Tekla (dog), 24, 25, 27
Teller, 33, 34
Thompson, Larry, 19
Thompson, Varona, 13, 15, 19-21, **19**, 23, 24, 28, 49
Tok, 18, 19
Tonzona River, 6
Topkok Hill, 32, 38, 44, 61
Torres, Frank, 60, 61, 62
Trabant, Evelyn, **15**
Trapper Creek, 45, 62, 65, 66

Turnagain Arm, 4, 6
Turnagain Mining District, 4

Uemura, Naomi, 51, 52
Unalakleet, 6, 7, 33, 36, 38, 55
Underwood, Nathan, 61

Vadla, Frances, 66
Vadla, Lars, 66
Valdez, 4
Vandiver, Shelley Gill (see Gill, Shelley)
Van Zyle, John, 52
Vaughan, Norman, 27, 28, 29, 38, 51, 52

Wagener, Joe, **51**
Walluk, David Race, 39
Wasilla-Knik Centennial Com., 12
Wendt, Ron, **66**
Whitehorse, Yukon, 49, 53, 59
White Mountain, 33, 34, 38, 57, 61
Wilk, Jane, 42
Wilk, Stan, 42
Willow, 57
Wilmarth, Dick, 13
Women's Sports Foundation, 35
 — Professional Sportswoman of the Year, 35
Wright, Gareth, 45, 46
Wright, Roxy, 44-45, **45**

Yentna River, 6, 25
Young, S. Hall, 6, 7
Yukon Quest Race, 16, 47, 48, 49, 53, 59
Yukon River, 3, 4, 5, 6, 29, 35, 50

Zagoskin, Lt., 3
Zamitykn, Vasily, 20